BROOKLYN'S
SPORTSMEN'S ROW

To Claudia,

He's the tale

of Sportsmen's Row

BROOKLYN'S
SPORTSMEN'S ROW

Politics, Society & the Sporting Life on Northern Eighth Avenue

LUCAS G. RUBIN

Charleston   London

THE
History
PRESS

Published by The History Press
Charleston, SC 29403
www.historypress.net

Images are courtesy of the author unless otherwise noted.

First published 2012

Manufactured in the United States

ISBN 978.1.60949.273.1

Library of Congress CIP data applied for.

CONTENTS

ACKNOWLEDGEMENTS

This book was possible only through the remarkable support and assistance of many colleagues, neighbors and friends. First and foremost, my deepest thanks to the Jockey Club's Edward Bowen for his consistent guidance and support. From the start, he generously made the world of horse racing and its storied traditions and institutions accessible. The New York Historical Society's Joseph Ditta is, without doubt, one of the most talented researchers with whom I have ever worked. I'm forever indebted to him for his assistance. My thanks, as well, to Liz Call at the Brooklyn Historical Society; Cathy Schenck of Keeneland Library; Ivy Marvel and Joy Holland at the Brooklyn Public Library's Brooklyn Collection; Carey Stumm, New York Transit Museum archivist; Carol Butler at Brown Brothers; Green-Wood Cemetery's Jane Cuccurullo; Alan Cohen of Cullen and Dykman LLP; and, of course, Whitney Tarella of The History Press, who found this project of sufficient merit. Walker Blankinship of Kensington Stables is owed two thanks: first, for keeping Brooklyn's storied equestrian tradition alive and second, for so generously sharing it with me. My brother-in-law, Michael Goldhaber, was a resource throughout. His formidable intellect, knowledge of the law and its traditions and mastery of the written word are virtually without peer. A thank you, as well, to all of my colleagues at Columbia University and particularly to John Genzale for making me an astute student of the business of sports. My thanks, as well, to all of the "brownstoners" for making the neighborhood what it is today, and my profound gratitude to those who specifically aided in this project: Charlie Brown, John Cassara, Clem Labine, Everett Ortner (*in memoriam*) and Bill Younger. A thanks to my mother (and map guru) Christina, Elise Burton and all of the Goldbergs for their love and support. More than thanks, I probably owe some apologies to all of the neighbors and unwitting pedestrians whom I endlessly talked up about the block's history. And finally, as with all things, my wife, Simona, and son, Itai, are my greatest strength and resource. My thanks to them for their patience, encouragement and enthusiastic support throughout.

INTRODUCTION

In Brooklyn of the 1890s, few addresses were more exclusive than those along Sportsmen's Row: the northernmost block of Eighth Avenue in the elite neighborhood of Park Slope. Named for its eponymous resident, the hall of fame jockey James McLaughlin, it subsequently became home to several titans of horse racing, including the jockey (and McLaughlin's hall of fame rival) Edward "Snapper" Garrison, the hall of fame horse trainer James Gordon Rowe Sr. and the "meteors of the racetrack," the brothers Michael and Philip Dwyer, who in twenty years went from being butchers who owned a single racehorse to being premier racetrack owners who owned a chain of meat markets.

But Sportsmen's Row also included a colorful array of other residents, a host of illuminati of the gaslight age including two leading vaudeville impresarios; the king of Brooklyn's late-night, free-wheeling saloon scene; two mayors; and (almost) one American president. It was an impressive collection. They say that sports is entertainment and that politics makes for strange bedfellows, and along Sportsmen's Row all three of these—sports, entertainment and politics—came together, literally, in surprising and novel ways: as partners in business, adversaries in court and rivals on the track.

This book is a brief history of all this and much more.

I first learned of Sportsmen's Row from my father, who knew only of its association with horse racing and that a mayor had once lived there. I later picked up various tidbits from many of the neighborhood's older

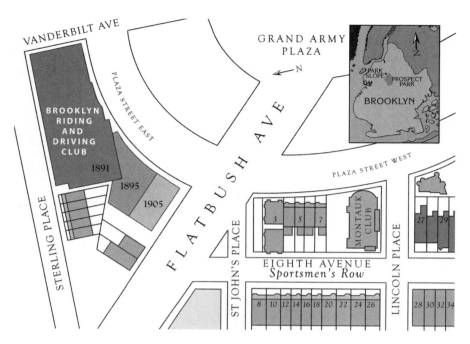

Sportsmen's Row and its immediate environs, 1905.

residents—that the jockeys of the block had stabled their horses just across Flatbush Avenue; that number 12 was the home of a Mrs. O'Dwyer, associated with an O'Dwyer stakes; and the oft-repeated identification of house number 22 as the residence of New York City mayor William Gaynor. In addition, I had long been intrigued by some of the block's more peculiar features—that all of the houses on its east side strangely face away from Eighth Avenue and that it is home to Brooklyn's only surviving Victorian-era social club.

In the summer of 2009, I began formally researching the history of Sportsmen's Row. My original goal was to simply verify some of what I had heard, but the more I investigated, the more interesting the story became—and the more it called for a more comprehensive telling. I soon found that much of what I had been told—the local oral "tradition," so to speak—was largely conjectural and, in some cases, downright apocryphal. Accordingly, my aim herein is to promulgate the historical record and, hopefully, to also convey some sense of (and reason for) its original celebrity and repute.

I had initially intended this to be a brief four- or five-chapter historical survey. In the end, an effective retelling required eight. Though the work remains essentially chronological, it necessarily incorporates one biographical and three topical chapters. Given the importance of William Gaynor (one of the block's *two* mayors), his presence could be given due justice only with its own chapter (Chapter 5). Similarly, the Brooklyn Jockey Club and its Gravesend racetrack were very much the focal point of the sportsmen—and many of their neighbors. Accordingly, they too are the focus of one entire chapter (Chapter 3). The Montauk Club also required a complete unit, not least because there has been surprisingly so little inquiry into its history (Chapter 6). Finally, the story of the long-lost Riding and Driving Club could be told only with its own chapter (Chapter 7); admittedly, its inclusion ultimately had more to do with it being such a fascinating piece of Brooklyn history than its actual significance to the block.

But first, a little something about the historical context in which Sportsmen's Row came to be.

The neighborhood of Park Slope was largely developed in the decades following the opening of Prospect Park in 1866.[1] New rail and streetcar lines came soon thereafter, while the inauguration of the Brooklyn Bridge in 1883 allowed for convenient travel to New York City. Affluent residents began moving to the area and, finding the avenues adjoining the park particularly desirable, built grand mansions and elegant town houses designed by the city's leading architects. By 1890, Park Slope was one of the wealthiest neighborhoods in the country.[2]

To nourish and sustain this burgeoning aristocracy, an infrastructure of "elite" institutions—such as social clubs, hospitals and private schools—was soon established. Social clubs played a central role in the cultural life of the nineteenth-century city, and Brooklyn, like all urban centers of note, had a good number of such organizations. While some catered to specific needs and interests (such as drama, the arts and athletics), almost all were geared toward an affluent, high-status male clientele. Although individuals frequently belonged to multiple clubs, location and shared ideologies (such as political party affiliation) were often motivating factors for joining. The major organizations generally possessed their own purpose-built clubhouses, and membership was tightly controlled.

It was also an era in which spectator sports were transforming from largely amateur phenomena to more professional and businesslike operations. To this end, governance and revenue generation became of

Grand Army Plaza, 1876. Northern Eighth Avenue is located to the far right. The large, empty thoroughfare is Union Street. *Courtesy of the Brooklyn Public Library, Brooklyn Collection.*

greater concern to owners and purveyors of athletic contests. Of these early spectator sports, one of the most popular was horse racing; in the latter decades of the 1800s, it was truly the sport of kings, drawing attendance on race days in the thousands, and its practitioners—the horses, jockeys, trainers and owners—were the sports icons of the age. Though now almost forgotten, Brooklyn, with its three great racetracks, was once at its very nexus.

This was the world in which Sportsmen's Row took shape. As for its specific origins, we begin at the very beginning.

ORIGINS, 1884–1891

O n an April morning in 1884, a reporter from the *New York Tribune* traveled to the corner of Eighth and Flatbush Avenues in the newly fashionable district of Prospect Heights.[3] Though he observed construction

James McLaughlin (center). *Courtesy of Keeneland-Hemment.*

throughout the neighborhood, he found this particular stretch of Eighth Avenue largely empty, its only features four new brownstone residences, numbers 20–26, and a stand of tall evergreens directly opposite. The reporter had come to this block to interview James McLaughlin, America's most famous jockey, who had just moved with his wife and three children to number 24.[4]

JAMES MCLAUGHLIN AND MICHAEL F. DWYER, NUMBERS 24 AND 26 EIGHTH AVENUE

The reporter stood before the houses, admiring their stately forms. They had been built in the previous year by owner-architect William Flanagan, an important early developer of the area. Though handsome, they were fairly typical for the period: classic four-story neo-Grecs with three-sided bay windows, topped with high cornices featuring alternating brackets and vertical fascia.[5] In front of number 24, the correspondent found a small boy helping a man fill a barrel with kindling as two young girls from the neighboring house looked on. The boy was McLaughlin's son, who, after some playful deception, directed the correspondent to ascend the stairs. At the door, the reporter was greeted by McLaughlin's wife, an attractive and fashionably dressed young woman. He took immediate note of the opulent entranceway, particularly its exterior doors of carved mahogany, colorful entrance foyer with inlaid marble and ornate brass gas lanterns.

Mrs. McLaughlin led the reporter to the parlor, which he found as elegant as the home's exterior. He was especially taken by the double drawing rooms, with their mahogany wainscoting, richly carved pocket doors and luxurious ornamentation. Jockey McLaughlin entered shortly thereafter, and after an exchange of pleasantries, the reporter complimented him on the beauty of the house and its furnishings. He made specific mention of the beautiful carpets, about which he noted, "Someone in the McLaughlin household has good taste to have chosen the carpet, which must have cost a pretty sum."

"That's a fact," responded McLaughlin, "it did cost a pretty sum. We have just been in here a week, and have only begun to furnish the place. I bought the house out and out and paid for it exactly twenty-five thousand

From the left: numbers 26 and 24 Eighth Avenue.

dollars cash down." Glancing around the room with a look of immense happiness, he added, "And I do think that my family are going to have a nice home."[6]

The house was also generously decorated with evidence of the jockey's many victories. A handsome piece of plate displayed in the center of the bay window was won at the Travers Stakes in 1881. There were also two trophies awarded by the *Sportsman*, one for winning the most money and the other for most victories in a season. Of particular pride to the jockey was a pair of antique silver spurs mounted on a plush velvet plaque. This was a prize from the Centennial Stakes, which he had won in 1881. The pair was, as McLaughlin noted, reminiscent of the old continental cavalry spurs used in the War of Independence and was once owned by an antebellum jockey named Rudd.

More than the jockey's Epicurean tastes, the paper's primary interest was in what made McLaughlin—"beyond a doubt, the favorite jockey of this country"—such a success. As McLaughlin indicated, "Well, I'm learning all the time. I love horses and study their dispositions." He also suggested that his salubrious lifestyle helped maintain his competitive edge and his weight: "I am always strong at the finish. You see, I neither chew, smoke nor drink, and I love my home and my business." He also offered up his fitness regimen: exercising horses early in the morning followed by a long, brisk walk (while wearing four heavy sweaters) and a diet of pure protein (roast meats and sirloin steaks) and nothing in the way of cake, pie, ice cream or, for that matter, vegetables. He was confident that his habits would help him always stay near his goal weight of 105 pounds, and—though at the time he was 128 pounds—he was unconcerned about being ready for the upcoming race season. It was an auspicious enough beginning to McLaughlin's life on Eighth Avenue.

That McLaughlin should end up in a grand town house in one of the city's most fashionable districts was a remarkable turn of affairs for a child born into extreme poverty in Hartford, Connecticut, on February 12, 1861.[7] Orphaned and homeless by his early teens, McLaughlin's fortune took a profound turn when he was taken in by one William "Father Bill" Daly (1839–April 3, 1931). Though ostensibly an owner and trainer of racehorses, Daly was far more successful in the cultivation of jockeys. His methods, though rough, were extraordinarily effective. Under Daly's strict tutelage, McLaughlin began riding competitively in the late 1870s and met with almost immediate success. On October 10, 1878, at Nashville, he became the first jockey to win an entire day's program, winning all three scheduled races. By 1880, he had become the chief jockey for the Dwyer brothers, whose stable was on its way to becoming a racing powerhouse. On their behalf, McLaughlin took the Kentucky Derby in 1881 on Hindoo, one of the great horses of the age.

The Dwyer brothers, on the other hand, had parlayed a successful business into a horse racing empire.[8] Michael (b. 1837) and his younger brother Philip (b. August 21, 1844) had made a fortune as butchers, owning five lucrative shops in downtown Brooklyn. From an interest in speedy delivery horses came one far more captivating to men of newfound riches: horse racing. Though they initially dabbled in trotters, Thoroughbreds soon became their passion. In August 1874, they purchased their first such horse, Rhadamanthus, from the renowned financier (and horse enthusiast) August Belmont Sr. (b. December 8, 1813). After Rhadamanthus took four of his first five races, the Dwyers committed their energies (and fortune) to the track. Always on the lookout for talent both equine and human, McLaughlin was a natural fit for the Dwyers' competitive instincts.

The Dwyers and McLaughlin spent a good portion of their time together at the track. Their wives, meanwhile, were the best of friends and nearly inseparable in their companionship.[9] And so, when McLaughlin purchased number 24, Mike Dwyer bought the adjoining residence at number 26; it was his daughters whom the reporter noted playing with McLaughlin's son before number 24. In addition to being elegant and well located, the houses were also within easy reach of the Brighton Beach and Sheepshead Bay racetracks, both of which were accessible via the Culver Line of the Prospect Park and Coney Island Railroad, the terminus of which was located to the south and served by a network of trolley and cab lines.

The auspicious start to McLaughlin's life on Eighth Avenue would hold true for his first few years in number 24—insomuch as his riding was concerned. He was the leading jockey from 1884 to 1887, won the Belmont Stakes six times between 1882 and 1888 and took the Preakness in 1885. At Monmouth in 1885, he repeated the feat of winning every race on the day's card, taking five first place finishes. The Dwyer Brothers Stable continued to provide him with champion Thoroughbreds, and the jockey seldom let them down. In all, they supplied him four future hall of fame horses: Hindoo, Hanover (Hindoo's offspring), Kingston and Luke Blackburn (whom McLaughlin considered the best horse he had ever ridden).

McLaughlin's successes meant further glory to his employers, whose colors (red with a blue sash) were now ubiquitous at all the major races. Though their operation was an unmitigated success, the brothers continued to seek new opportunities for financial gain. Inveigled by their growing wealth and prestige, they ultimately concluded that ownership of a racetrack would be far more profitable than merely owning racehorses. Accordingly, in the winter of 1885–86, they organized the Brooklyn Jockey Club and built a racetrack that spring and summer over the old Prospect Park Fair Grounds in Gravesend.

While Phil became president of the club and managed its day-to-day affairs, Mike preferred to occupy himself with gambling on the races; he was soon considered one of the greatest "plungers" of the era, whose regular wagers easily climbed into the tens of thousands.[10] Away from the excitement of the track, however, Mike Dwyer's life on Eighth Avenue was far from what the public might have imagined. He belonged to no clubs, attended few social events and seldom engaged the company of others. Rather, he spent most of his time at home with his wife, Louise, and their five children.[11]

Jockey McLaughlin, on the other hand, never quite adjusted to the mundane pleasures of domesticity.[12] By the spring of 1888, he had begun to falter on the track, having opened the season overweight and unable to find his rhythm in the saddle. He appeared lethargic, distracted and—worst of all—lacking in competitive spirit. To compound matters, the Dwyer Stable was also floundering, having failed to secure any champion horses close to the caliber of Hanover, who was nearing retirement. By late May, McLaughlin's riding was simply dreadful, notably having failed to take even second place while riding the still potent Hanover on Saturday the twenty-third. The troubles reached a boiling point the following Tuesday when Mike Dwyer and McLaughlin got into a shouting match at the Gravesend racetrack. The incident nearly came to blows, with McLaughlin exclaiming, "You're a nice man to attempt to strike me after I have ridden you [to] nearly $1,000,000."[13] The jockey stormed off, and the Dwyers subsequently dismissed his valet, Charles Le Ponce. This much the public knew.

What was less generally known was that McLaughlin's personal life had been in tatters for much of the previous year. He had not made his residence on Eighth Avenue for quite some time and, having spent the past winter at the Clarendon Hotel in Brooklyn, was now living at the Dwyer Brothers Stable at the Gravesend track. The passion and energy that the jockey had once brought to the track was now obsessively focused on one Libbie King, a racing "groupie" whom McLaughlin had first met at the Monmouth Park racetrack in 1885. The wife of a postal employee, a contemporary source described her as "a blond by bleachery, [who] had more vivacity than beauty, but she dressed stylishly and commanded general attention wherever she went."[14]

Mrs. McLaughlin had actually harbored suspicions about her husband's infidelity for some time. In July 1887, her worst fears were confirmed when she discovered a collection of incriminating letters. She immediately departed number 24, swearing that she would neither file for divorce nor ever live with McLaughlin again. In the months that followed, Louise Dwyer devoted herself to engineering a rapprochement, even managing to arrange an awkward meeting between the two couples. Through her tireless efforts, she eventually secured a commitment of renewed loyalty from the jockey and a willingness to seek reconciliation from Mrs. McLaughlin.

The accord, however, proved short-lived. That May, shortly before the altercation with Mike Dwyer at the track, McLaughlin was served with papers by his paramour's husband, who was seeking $25,000 in damages for the alienation of his wife's affections. Le Ponce, the jockey's valet, later told the papers that this was the reason for the fight and not McLaughlin's wretched riding the previous Saturday. He also went on to blame Mrs. McLaughlin for the troubles, stating that she was using her influence to create the ill will. For their part, the Dwyers claimed that La Ponce was a negative influence and responsible for McLaughlin's "lack of training and mode of living."[15]

The marriage was irretrievably broken, and McLaughlin's aggrieved wife returned with their three children to her family home in Connecticut. The contents of number 24, once so carefully selected and thoughtfully displayed, were promptly sold off. As part of the divorce settlement, the former Mrs. McLaughlin received a $15,000 mortgage on the house that would pay her 6 percent interest through 1892.

Jockey McLaughlin and the Dwyer brothers managed to patch up their relationship enough to stay together through the end of the summer, ultimately parting ways on August 28, 1888. At least publicly, the Dwyers refrained from tarnishing the jockey and offered nothing but kind words and well wishes. McLaughlin, on the other hand, felt the stigma of the whole sordid incident and penned something of a clumsy self-exculpation for the September 2 *New York Tribune*:

> *I would like the public distinctly to understand once* [and] *for all that there is not, nor has there been, a woman to cause the separation between the Dwyer Brothers and myself. It was simply a disagreement on both sides. We had each decided to make a change sooner or later. If their horses lacked the speed of former years, if the training was unsatisfactory, and if in their*

races they met as good or better horses, I could hardly be expected to do more than my best to pilot them to victory. But in my failure to win it is hardly just to say that I am losing my form in riding through any domestic troubles.

He concluded by blaming his ex-wife and her friends for the gossip; he undoubtedly meant Louise Dwyer. Of the whole affair, the *Times-Union* of Brooklyn noted: "It's all right when a woman gets stuck on a jockey, but when a jockey gets stuck on a woman then its wrong. [That] seems to be the trouble here."[16]

McLaughlin, now a public jockey, left that September for the racetracks of Chicago. He retired from racing in 1892, unable to stay at a competitive weight. Thereafter, he became a trainer and racing official. He died on January 19, 1927, in New Orleans, where he had gone to serve as a patrol judge. In 1955, he was voted, along with his old mount Hindoo, into the inaugural class of the National Museum of Racing and Hall of Fame at Saratoga. Ironically, McLaughlin's daughter ended up marrying someone quite like her father: the jockey Thomas (Tommy) Burns, who was also a protégé of Father Bill. Burns was the leading rider in 1898 and 1899 and also raced for a number of years in Europe. He was tragically struck and killed by a train on November 15, 1913. Unlike his father in law, Burns's obituary made specific note of his happy domestic life.[17] In 1983, he too was inducted into the National Museum of Racing and Hall of Fame.

ALFRED CHAPIN, NUMBER 24 EIGHTH AVENUE

At the time of McLaughlin's departure, Prospect Heights was reaching the apex of desirability.[18] Grand residences, designed by the city's leading architects—including C.P.H. Gilbert, Montrose Morris, Helme & Huberty and the Parfitt Brothers—were erected along Plaza Street and Ninth (now Prospect Park West) and lower Eighth Avenues, rapidly filling in the last remaining open spaces. Their new residents were predominantly men of self-made wealth who had found success in industry, business, trade and banking. They included the industrialist J. Rogers Maxwell (78 Eighth Avenue, built 1883); the chewing gum king Thomas Adams Jr. (number 115, 1888); the shoe manufacturer John Hanan (number 118, 1890); Charles Feltman, inventor of the hot dog (number 130, circa 1890); and George C. Tilyou, builder of

Coney Island's Steeplechase Park (35 Prospect Park West, circa 1890). There was also a smattering of Brooklyn's more traditional aristocracy, some of whom traced their ancestry to the earliest Dutch families.

Prominent among these new arrivals was a host of Democratic politicians, a virtual who's-who of local legislative authority who established a party stronghold in the area.[19] One such politician with interest in the neighborhood was Brooklyn's young Democratic mayor, Alfred Chapin (b. March 8, 1848; in office 1888–91). In January 1889, he was riding in his coach along Eighth Avenue when he spied the now vacant number 24. The location was ideal and the house appropriate for a man of his station. After examining its interior, he immediately determined to buy it.[20]

The mayor dispatched an assistant to negotiate with the broker, C.N. Moody. The asking price for the house was $30,000, but Chapin's representative was both persistent and persuasive, and the sum of $23,000 was eventually agreed upon. The mayor was so eager to move into the jockey's house that he immediately closed on the sale of his own home in nearby Clinton Hill. The residents of Eighth Avenue were elated to welcome someone of the mayor's stature, while the mayor was equally delighted to

Eighth Avenue and Carroll Street from the south (circa 1905). Clockwise from the lower left are the Feltman, Hannan and Adams mansions.

Alfred Chapin. *Courtesy of Print Collection, Miriam and Ira D. Wallach Division of Arts, Prints and Photographs, New York Public Library.*

take his place along Sportsmen's Row—a sobriquet first made official by the January 27, 1889 *Brooklyn Daily Eagle* as "Sporting Men's Row" and subsequently by the February 5 edition as "Sportsmen's Row."

The sale, however, ran into one snag: the former Mrs. McLaughlin. A title search uncovered that she—now going by her maiden name, Pillon—was the holder of the $15,000 mortgage on number 24. At the time, she was living in a small residence on Seventh Avenue, having returned from her self-imposed exile in Connecticut. A sales agent visited her at her home and, informing her of the sale, presented her with a check covering the total. This she promptly refused, informing the agent:[21]

> *I hold a mortgage upon one of the most valuable pieces of property in the city…if I should sign a release now and accept the principal I should lose $2,700 (i.e. three years of interest). I do not see why I should lose that sum simply to oblige the Mayor and my husband, and I refuse to do so.*

Money probably had little to do with her stubborn refusal, as Ms. Pillon came from some means. Rather, this was about causing further embarrassment to her ex-husband. Though the mayor had nothing to do with their marital discord, he was now in something of a bind, having already sold his own home. When asked by a reporter from the *Brooklyn Daily Eagle* about the stalled sale, he responded, "I have not heard of any trouble. You will have to ask somebody else." Before turning to depart, he added, "You cannot make anyone release a mortgage, can you?"[22]

Behind the scenes, the mayor's counsel and agents from Moody scrambled to salvage the sale. Both Mayor Chapin and Jockey McLaughlin were adamant in their refusal to pay her the additional $2,700 above the principal. A couple days later, however, she acquiesced for an additional $1,000, and the transaction was finalized. That May, Mayor Chapin took his place along Sportsmen's Row. On the occasion, he was feted by the nascent Montauk Club on Thursday, May 16, in its temporary clubhouse at 34 Eighth Avenue.[23]

With Chapin now firmly ensconced in his new home, he was free to regale his new neighbors with "narratives of his triumphs in the form of debate," and they—Mike Dwyer, to be specific—could "respond by telling of the performances of the Brooklyn Racing Stable, from Hindoo and Luke Blackburn down to the equine wonders of a later period."[24]

"THE PRESIDENT WON'T BECOME A BROOKLYN MAN"

Chapin's move to Sportsmen's Row set something of a precedent, as political power would now become a factor in the emerging fabric of Sportsmen's Row. The mayor's addition also brought the reputation of the area as a Democratic stronghold to even greater heights, so much so that rumors began to swirl that President Grover Cleveland himself, whose term was ending that year, was considering a move to the neighborhood.[25] In anticipation, C.N. Moody and William Gubbins, a prominent local builder, formally offered the president newly built number 27 Eighth Avenue. The suggested price was $36,000, and the residence, a beautiful Romanesque Revival mansion constructed of atypical yellow Euclid stone, was considered one of the finest on the hill.

Hopes for such a move were ultimately dashed by a letter from the president's secretary, received at the offices of C.N. Moody on February 12:[26]

> *Dear Sirs—The President has received your recent letter, but his plans for his residence in New York City are so far matured that he does not desire to consider the matter to which you call his attention.*
> *Very respectfully, D.S. Lamont, Private Secretary*

Cleveland did in fact go on to spend the next few years working as a lawyer in the neighboring metropolis and eventually completed a second term as chief executive (1893–97). On the eve of the 1892 election, October 21, he was a guest of honor at the Montauk Club, whose new clubhouse stood just across the street from number 27.[27] There is no doubt that many of those in attendance—that veritable phalanx of Democrats who now called Prospect Heights home—wondered what might have been had Cleveland been so inclined to join their ranks. As it were, the president eventually retired to his home state of New Jersey.

The lovely 27 Eighth Avenue. Unfortunately, President Cleveland wasn't interested.

EDWARD "SNAPPER" GARRISON, NUMBER 30 EIGHTH AVENUE

A month after Chapin moved into Jockey McLaughlin's former home, Sportsmen's Row gained another renowned man of the turf when the jockey Edward "Snapper" Garrison purchased number 30 Eighth Avenue for $17,000.[28] Like McLaughlin—who was also a frequent competitor on the turf—Garrison was one of the most successful and famous riders of the 1880s.[29]

Edward Henry Garrison was born on February 9, 1868, in New Haven. At the age of ten, he began working as a blacksmith's apprentice, where he developed an interest in horses. Like McLaughlin, he also came to the attention of "Father Bill" Daly, who subsequently provided Garrison both a career and a nickname: "Jack Snapper," on account of his "wiry activity and his alertness."[30] While the "Jack" never stuck, the "Snapper" did—and helped make him a household name. At the age of twelve, he competed in his first race.

Garrison's belletristic countenance masked a fiercely competitive nature, which manifested the instant he donned his racing silks. In 1883, his first major year on the circuit, he literally burst onto the scene, taking five of six consecutive races at Brighton Beach that August. In 1886, while riding Dutch Roller for the celebrated owner James R. Keene, Garrison pulled off a legendary feat at the Great Eastern Handicap, subsequently memorialized with a metaphor. At the race, contested over three-quarters of a mile at the Sheepshead Bay racetrack, Garrison broke last in a field of twenty-four. He trailed the field through the home stretch, whereupon he exhorted his mount to drive headlong through the crowd of leading horses, winning by a wide margin. The finish was so astounding that the crowd was swept off its feet, and the "Garrison Finish" became the embodiment of the come-from-behind victory. It was dramatic, tense and daring—and perfectly suited to Garrison's style.

Throughout the 1880s, Garrison rode for a series of owners, earning more for his services with each passing season. In the two years preceding his move to Sportsmen's Row, he racked up victories in 1887 at Monmouth Oaks and the Jerome Handicap and in 1888 at the Champion Stakes, Coney Island Derby, Freehold Stakes, Monmouth Handicap and also repeated at the Jerome Handicap.

Edward "Snapper" Garrison. *Courtesy of Keeneland Library.*

At the same time, he met with success off the turf. In 1886, he married Sadie McMahon, the attractive and engaging daughter of Judge William McMahon. The judge, like many members of the social elite, had both a passion for horse racing and the money with which to indulge it. Garrison and McMahon subsequently organized a racing venture under the auspices of McMahon & Co., for which the jockey was a silent partner. Their efforts were initially quite successful and produced several winning horses, including the Thoroughbreds Cyclops and Eolian.

At the time of his purchase of number 30, Garrison had just become the chief rider for August Belmont Sr. The terms of employment were lucrative, and though Garrison had been living nearby at 91 Sixth Avenue, the increased remuneration undoubtedly prompted his decision to move farther up the hill and take his place on Sportsmen's Row. Life was good for Garrison in 1889, and Sportsmen's Row was the perfect place to showcase his newfound wealth, status and success.

Garrison's new home had been built in 1881–82 as one in a series of four (including 32, 34 and 38; there is no 36) by local owner-architect-builder J. Doherty. An attractive flush-front neo-Grec brownstone, its façade is wonderfully articulated by a series of large, boldly framed windows and crowned by an attractive wrought-iron roof cresting atop its cornice.[31] The Garrisons brought to their new house an impressive collection of opulent furniture and luxury accoutrements, including an upholstered Turkish parlor set, full mahogany library, solid mahogany bedroom set (with hair mattress), maple secretary and all manner of silverware, clocks, bronzes and fine carpets. Garrison was also a terrific pool player, and his prized Brunswick and Balk Billiard Combination table was to occupy a prominent position in the double parlors. After moving in, he had the front stepping stone engraved with the initials "E.H.G." and a mat lettered "E.G." placed in the entrance vestibule.

At the time Garrison was taking up residence in number 30, plans were also afoot to establish two premier social clubs within the ambit of Sportsmen's Row: the Montauk and the Brooklyn Riding and Driving Clubs. The placement of the Montauk Club at 25 Eighth Avenue—literally across the street from the homes of Chapin and Mike Dwyer—well demonstrates the importance of northern Eighth Avenue,[32] as does the location of the Riding and Driving Club, which was built on a parcel of land just across the terminus of Eighth Avenue, perpendicular to Flatbush Avenue. When completed, the two clubs would essentially "bookend" the block.

Number 30 Eighth Avenue.

JAMES G. ROWE, NUMBER 12 EIGHTH AVENUE

In April 1891, James Gordon Rowe Sr. purchased the newly built number 12 Eighth Avenue for $18,000.[33] Number 12 was one of four brownstones erected in 1890 by owner-builder William Gubbins (who had earlier tried to sell number 27 Eighth Avenue to President Cleveland). At three and a half stories, it is a simple, if elegant, neo-Grec structure that was built as a twin of number 14. Numbers 16 and 18 were also built as twins, though in the Romanesque style.[34] Upon their completion, Gubbins would take up residence in number 16.

To the burgeoning fame of Sportsmen's Row, Rowe brought even further cachet.[35] Born in 1857 in the outskirts of Richmond, Virginia, at the age of ten, he came under the apprenticeship of the famed owner and trainer Colonel David McDaniel. Under the colonel's guidance, the successes came fast and early for Rowe: legend holds that his first victory earned him peppermint candy and permission to stay up until 9:00 p.m. Between 1871 and 1873, he was the nation's leading jockey, including a victory at the 1872 Saratoga Cup astride Harry Bassett. After growing too large to race, he became a professional stunt rider, most notably performing in P.T. Barnum's Great Roman Hippodrome in New York City.

By 1876, Rowe had become a trainer, and in 1878 he became the trainer for the Dwyer brothers, for whom he subsequently trained seven champion racehorses: Bramble (1879), Luke Blackburn (1880), Onondaga (1881), Hindoo (1881, 1882), George Kinney (1882, 1883), Runnymede (1882) and Miss Woodford (1883, 1884). Rowe abruptly left the Dwyer stable in September 1884 in protest over the brothers' insistence on running Miss Woodford, whom Rowe believed to have a leg injury. Though the Dwyers had a reputation for overworking their horses, Rowe found their demands in this instance to be unconscionable (Miss Woodford ultimately ran, with McLaughlin as her jockey, and won by two lengths).

After leaving the Dwyers, Rowe trained for several other owners, eventually coming under the employ of August Belmont Sr. by 1888.[36] Together with Snapper Garrison in his service, Belmont had assembled something of a turf "dream team." Rowe had also "made it"—training for one of the elite men (even if a *novus homo*) of New York. In 1889–90, the triad turned out several champions, most notably taking the 1889 Suburban Handicap with Raceland. Their time together, however, proved quite short. On November 24, 1890, Belmont died of heart failure. That final year together was the most profitable in Belmont's long tenure as a Thoroughbred owner: $125,636 in earnings and the only time that his take actually covered his racing expenses.

Number 12 Eighth Avenue.

Rowe's move to number 12 seems to correspond with something of a surprising career change. After Belmont's death, he became a starter. Before electric starting gates (which became widespread after 1939), starting was by and large a manual process. The starter, standing on a platform alongside the horses and jockeys, dropped a flag to signal the start of the race. The system was clumsy and, in a sport where every second mattered, fraught with numerous problems of accuracy. Though the starter had some assistance with the process (such as a forward spotter to identify false starts), equitability in matters of adjudication was challenging—and subjective. While lacking the sexiness or potential fame and financial reward of training, the position was critically important in the early days of the sport, and starters were generally well compensated.

At the time of Rowe's hire, horse racing was undergoing a critical professional evolution. Previous to 1891, there was no national governing body for the sport by which to maintain and enforce uniformity of standards, policies and regulation. In February 1891, the Board of Control was formed in New York City with the purpose of providing such governance. Of its seven members, four were track owners and included Phil Dwyer on behalf of the Brooklyn Jockey Club. Though the Board of Control would ultimately be merged in 1894 into a new authority, the Jockey Club, it was nonetheless a bold evolution in the professionalization of the sport. It was the newly established Board of Control that officially licensed Rowe as a starter. For its part, it was a smart choice: the former trainer was deeply respected in the industry and a consummate, hardworking professional. As the December 29, 1890 *New York Times* offered, "The race courses have need of good starters, and Mr. Rowe will be a welcome addition to the ranks."

Ironically, the position also brought Rowe back into the Dwyer racing operation, as he was appointed official starter of the Brooklyn Jockey Club. Although not necessarily reporting to his former employers, he was at least working closely with them—and, not to mention, his handling of the flag would have its impact on their races.

MIKE DWYER, NUMBER 26 EIGHTH AVENUE

In his capacity as a starter, Rowe would be engaging a markedly different Dwyer operation. In August 1890, the brothers had formally dissolved their racing partnership.[37] At the time, Phil had explained to the press:[38]

My brother Mike and I have contemplated dissolving partnership for several years, but never really saw our way clear to doing [so] until this season. The desire for the dissolution was mutual, and the only cause for breaking up the firm is the desire that each of us has to be perfectly independent and to buy or sell horses as each may think fit without having to consult with the other.

The dissolution came as little surprise. Following McLaughlin's departure, the stable had continued to perform poorly, and there had been rumors of an impending split for the previous two years. The brothers and their famous "Dwyer Luck" had been unable to match their earlier successes in a sport that was becoming increasingly professional and more competitive. Their earlier strategy of purchasing proven winners had also become increasingly more difficult, and they were not finding success in running out younger horses of known pedigree but unproven talent.

The brothers' time together, however, had been extraordinarily successful—particularly their years with McLaughlin. They had collected some $1,500,000 in purses; headed the list of winning owners in 1881, 1882, 1883, 1885 and 1887; owned the winningest horse (Hanover) and mare (Miss Woodford) to date; and won nearly every famous American race save the Suburban and Brooklyn Handicaps. It was an impressive resume. Following their separation, Phil went into partnership with his son Philip Jr. under the auspices of Dwyer & Son.

When reporters went to number 26 to ask Mike about the split, they were informed that he was too ill to speak with them. It may have been no idle dismissal. Mike had in fact been in poor health for much of the previous two years of the failing partnership. His gambling, always problematic, might have had a negative impact on his health; it was certainly rumored to have played a role in the demise of the Dwyer Brothers Stable. Speculation as to the cause of his poor health was rampant. One elderly turfman, lounging in the art gallery of the St. James Hotel, relayed to the *New York Tribune* that Mike Dwyer in fact had a rather unusual drinking problem:[39]

I can't say that I ever saw Mike take a drink, but I am convinced that he is drinking himself to death…Mike Dwyer has the mineral water mania. In his brownstone house in Brooklyn he has a room stacked with the waters of all the famous springs of the world. If he hears of a new mineral water discovery…he proceeds forthwith to lay in a few barrels…He is suffering from a somewhat peculiar malady which he imagines some sort of mineral water is going to cure, and he will leave no stone unturned to find it...I hate to think of such a man drinking himself to death. Look at Phil: He doesn't drink much water.

Mike Dwyer, however, wasn't the only one in the house in poor health. Louise had also been ill for some time, and her doctors eventually suspected something far worse than mineral water mania: stomach cancer.[40] Soon after Rowe purchased number 12, she underwent a surgical procedure from which she contracted sepsis and died several days later (June 2). She was thirty-nine years old. Immediately after she passed, wires were sent out to the tracks, and no Dwyer horses were run that day.

A memorial service for her was held that Thursday.[41] Following a laying out at number 26, a funeral cortege departed at 10:00 a.m. for St. Francis Xavier Church, at the corner of Carroll Street and Sixth Avenue. Though the family had asked for no flowers, hundreds of mourners sent along funeral bouquets, which filled the church. The pastor eulogized the deceased as kind-hearted, generous and warm, and the church's choir performed a solemn high mass by Cherubini and sang "Nearer My God to Thee." Among those present were Mr. and Mrs. Chapin, Snapper Garrison and his wife and a host of other residents of northern Eighth Avenue. Representatives of all the racing clubs, tracks and organizations were also in attendance. Following the service, Louise's body was interred in the Cemetery of the Holy Cross.

Mike Dwyer was absolutely devastated by his wife's death. As the June 3 *New York Times* noted, he "had the heartfelt sympathy of even his enemies, all of whom knew him as a man whose domestic life was a charming one." He would never quite be the same again.

PHILIP J. DWYER, NUMBER 8 EIGHTH AVENUE

Though no longer working together, the Dwyer brothers still maintained a close fraternal bond and a shared interest in the Brooklyn Jockey Club. With Mike now deeply depressed and physically unwell, Phil sought to join him on Sportsmen's Row. In September 1891, he submitted plans to build a new house on the last open lot on the block—on the end opposite his brother, at the corner of Eighth Avenue and St. John's Place.[42]

From the left: numbers 10 and 8 Eighth Avenue.

The house that Phil Dwyer would erect would be the largest on the block, truly unique in structure and scale. It was designed by local architect John Mumford, who was best known for his work on several large public buildings, including Brooklyn's first Municipal Building and the original Methodist Episcopal Hospital.[43] The building actually consists of a matched pair of residences (numbers 8 and 10), standing five stories tall. It is a Romanesque confection, with a steep slate roof and bay windows standing atop colonnaded logia. The building originally had two adjacent stoops, which turned in opposite directions at their landings. It cost $31,000 to construct.

Mumford had been a navy draughtsman during the Civil War and had drawn plans for every U.S. Navy monitor save that of the eponymous *Monitor*. This is notable, as both numbers 8 and 10 have some strikingly peculiar features that evoke the "feel" of a naval vessel. Their original main hallways, for instance, at one point taper to form a square that evokes the narrow confines of a ship's hold.

In December 1892, Phil moved from nearby Carleton Street to his new home on Eighth Avenue. With Garrison, Rowe and both Dwyers now all making their residence on Sportsmen's Row, the block had genuinely earned its nickname. By the time of Phil's arrival, however, the seeds of its dissolution as a nexus of elite sportsmen had already taken root.

2

THE SPORTSMEN, 1892–1900

S ometime in the winter of 1891–92, a city assessor made his way along
Eighth Avenue, estimating the value of the surrounding homes and
properties. He walked up and down the block, making careful note of the
changed streetscape and new homes. Though some effort had been made to
standardize the manner by which he was assessing value, the process was still
very much subjective.

When he arrived on the stretch between St. John's and Lincoln Places, he
would have found a block markedly enhanced from that just the year before.
The west side of the street was almost entirely built up with fine brownstone
mansions, the grand clubhouse of the Montauk Club now dominated the
southeast side and just across Flatbush, beyond an undeveloped lot, stood
the monumental stable of the recently completed Riding and Driving Club.
It was an impressive sight. The assessor was also wholly aware of the block
and its famed residents. By that winter, its moniker had become quite well
known: Sportsmen's Row, home to the titans of the turf.

Property valuation was going up throughout the city—higher taxes, of
course—and Sportsmen's Row would subsequently play a prominent role
in the coverage.[44] The June 21 *Brooklyn Daily Eagle* followed the occurrence
under the headline "The Row Raised: Eighth Avenue Property Valuation
Increased": "On Eighth and Ninth Avenue, the aristocratic park slope, the
work of increase is seen. Take Sportsmen's Row, on Eighth Avenue, for
example, and see what the assessing committee there has done." The houses
of Chapin (number 24), Rowe (number 12) and Mike Dwyer (number 26)

Looking northwest onto Plaza Street, post 1905. The Montauk Club is visible toward the top in the center and Sportsmen's Row immediately behind. *Courtesy of the Brooklyn Public Library, Brooklyn Collection.*

were all specifically cited, with Chapin's house raised to $17,000 (from $16,000) and Dwyer's to $21,000 (from $19,000).[45]

With the local reputation of Sportsmen's Row firmly established, that of the larger block would soon reach a national audience. In April 1893, Julian Ralph, an acclaimed journalist and occasional travel writer, would pen a guide to Brooklyn in *Harper's New Monthly Magazine*. He painted a picture of a vibrant and bustling city, but one that ultimately lived in the shadow of the neighboring metropolis: a city of the great "married middle" whose residents were, generally speaking, "far more interested in New York than in Brooklyn. They do not know in which ward they live, they cannot name the sheriff or their members of assembly, and in politics the only local episodes that stir them are the contests for the mayoralty." He also surveyed the city's various neighborhoods, offering a mix of their history and general character: "Another among the new and attractive residence districts is the Park Slope section, where, on Eighth and Ninth avenues, are many houses of considerable showiness, more closely built, but revealing the varied individual tastes of the owners." It was here that "a DuMaurier [a British cartoonist] might find new grist for his pencil, because those who enjoy the fruits of generations of refinement find as neighbors such nouveaux riches as a millionaire chewing gum manufacturer, the leading jockey of America, his most ambitious rival on the turf, a pawnbroker and a milliner."

Not surprisingly, the article caused something of a sensation.[46] Umbrage was taken with many of its remarks, most particularly that Brooklyn was presented as the "great sleeping-room" of New York (and for being quite self-conscious about it). The reference to the nouveaux riche of Park Slope also provoked ire, not least because self-made men were an American tradition. Ralph's selection of Eighth Avenue residents was, however, quite clever and not entirely unrepresentative. The chewing gum manufacturer was Thomas Adams Jr. (number 115); the pawnbroker was probably Samuel Goodstein (number 41); and the milliner was Joseph Wechsler (number 31). The jockeys were, of course, Garrison and McLaughlin; though not contemporaries on Sportsmen's Row, they were certainly rivals on the track. It was a colorful mix.

An anonymous letter writer to the *Knoxville* [Tennessee] *Sentinel*, of all places, offered up a vigorous defense of Adams ("a charitable and learned man belonging to several Brooklyn societies for the promotion of the arts and sciences") and took issue with the fact that he was lumped together with a pawnbroker and two jockeys.[47] This is telling, in part, for its attitude toward class and profession; for all of the romance and celebrity of the track, many still considered it déclassé. On March 31, the *Brooklyn Daily Eagle* dispatched a reporter to seek comment from those mentioned in the article. At number 115, Thomas Adams's son John was shown the letter and asked, "Have you any idea who your champion in Knoxville is?"

"No," he replied. "I do not know anyone there. I do not understand this exactly." Neither Goodstein nor Wechsler was home. At number 30, the house was dark, as Garrison was away in Florida. The *Eagle* also sought comment from Rowe and Mike Dwyer, but neither was in. Of McLaughlin, the paper noted that he had once lived on the block but that he was no longer listed in the city directory.

Generally lost within the hubbub was that Ralph's article was generally quite laudatory of Brooklyn. Ralph had lived for a time in the city and was quite familiar with his subject.[48] It was where he had first established his journalistic credentials, covering the trial of Henry Ward Beecher in 1875 for the *New York Daily Graphic*. Ralph would subsequently cover the trial of Lizzie Borden in June 1893 and later become a war correspondent for the *London Daily Mail* during the Second Boer War, where he was an eyewitness to the capture of Pretoria in 1900.

THE DWYERS, NUMBERS 8 AND 26 EIGHTH AVENUE

In the same month that Brooklyn's Eighth Avenue came to the nation's attention and the city wrestled with Julian Ralph's perceived slight, Mike Dwyer sold his house to James Troy, a celebrated ex-judge, for $32,500. The reason for his departure was entirely therapeutic: number 26 was haunted with too many memories of his beloved wife.[49] Dwyer moved to 45 West Eighty-third Street in New York City, where he became the neighbor of Richard Croker, the boss of Tammany Hall, the city's nefarious political machine. Dwyer had not turned his sights on politics but rather had developed a professional relationship with Croker in the ownership of racehorses.

Mike would soon return to Sportsmen's Row, now provided with a happy occasion: the marriage of Phil's nineteen-year-old daughter, Lydia.[50] When Phil had first moved with his family to number 8, he sold the adjoining residence (number 10) to the brothers William and Robert Furey. William was the commissioner of jurors, while his brother Robert was a contractor by trade. Robert was also a partner in the firm that held the citywide contract for cleaning the streets. The firm owed its success to the involvement of alderman James McGarry, who, though his office prevented him from receiving a public contract, had installed his wife, Bridget, as a partner in the firm. Their twenty-one-year-old-son son, Joseph, was also appointed the firm's chief clerk. It was a lucrative contract, and both Furey and the McGarrys benefitted handsomely.

Joseph was a frequent visitor to number 10, and it was there that love blossomed with the attractive, slender daughter of the racing titan who lived next door. The two were soon engaged, and on the morning of Thursday, June 29, 1893, they were married at the Church of St. Augustine before a circle of prominent sportsmen and politicians. The wedding party included Camille Dwyer, Lydia's sister and maid of honor, and Philip Dwyer Jr., the best man. When the ceremony concluded, the newlyweds were chauffeured to Grand Central Station, where they left to honeymoon in Chicago. As a present, Phil gave his daughter and son-in-law the deed to number 8 Eighth Avenue.

At the wedding, many of the guests would have been delighted to see Phil Jr. playing a significant role. When he had first partnered with his father, Phil Jr. had been integral to their new racing operation. Though young, he was talented and hardworking. He had grown up around horses and had early on demonstrated an aptitude for their cultivation. As a boy, he had helped exercise the horses at the Dwyer Brothers Stable, and he later rode them in time trials. He once even donned the Dwyer Brothers' racing colors, driving Belle B to a second place finish at the Gravesend track. He was a logical and ideal partner for his father's new venture.

In the year before his sister's wedding, however, his lungs had begun to trouble him, and he was increasingly absent from the stable. His doctors diagnosed consumption (tuberculosis) and sent him to Florida to recuperate. The humid clime seemed to improve his health, and he was doing well enough to return home for his sister's wedding in June. By that November, however, his health had deteriorated again, and his family sent him to Los Angeles to convalesce. He never recovered his strength and died at the Westminster Hotel on December 15.[51] Phil, who had come to visit him, was by his side. He was twenty-two years old.

The body was returned east, and a funeral was held on December 23 at the Church of St. Augustine, where his sister Lydia had been married only six months before.[52] After gathering at number 8, a funeral procession made its way to the church. There, Phil Jr.'s brothers, Charles and James, presented a large floral cross and the McGarry family a memorial wreath. Following a viewing, the body was interred in the family plot at the Cemetery of the Holy Cross. There was a large attendance at the funeral, including many renowned sportsmen, politicians and Eighth Avenue neighbors. Among those noted were the Furey brothers and Snapper Garrison.

SNAPPER GARRISON, NUMBER 30 EIGHTH AVENUE

At the time Garrison sat in mourning in a pew at St. Augustine, another turf record was shortly on his horizon. He was about to be offered a retainer of $23,500 for the upcoming racing year, the highest amount offered any jockey to date. He had also entertained competing offers from three other owners (including his old mentor, Daly). The years since Garrison had moved to Sportsmen's Row had corresponded, much like McLaughlin before him, with his greatest success as a rider. In that time, he had competed in all the major races of the East, notably taking one Belmont Stakes (with Foxford in 1891), one Realization Stakes (in 1892 on Tammany, his favorite mount) and the Jerome Handicap for the third time (1892). In 1892, he also took his second Suburban Handicap at Sheepshead Bay in spectacular fashion: a Garrison Finish, of course.

On June 24, 1893, Garrison pulled off his most daring victory, riding Boundless in a $50,000 stake at the American Derby in Chicago (during the World's Fair, no less). He skillfully manipulated the start of the race, feigning trouble with his strap and saddle, mounting and dismounting the horse and leaning on the side rail—all the time providing Boundless with sufficient rest. In so doing, he managed to delay the start of the race by more than an hour. When the race finally began, he won by eight lengths before a crowd of 100,000. Though he was fined $1,000 for his actions, the results stood, and Garrison's reputation for boldness and chutzpah reached new heights.

Garrison's last competitive year in the saddle was 1895, when he rode for Colonel Jacob Ruppert. Ruppert (b. August 5, 1867) was the wealthy scion of a brewing family who would go on to establish his own legacy as New York State congressman (1899–1907) and later as owner of the New York Yankees, which he would purchase in 1915. Ruppert would own the Yankees until his death (January 13, 1939), building the first Yankee Stadium (1923) and establishing a franchise ethos deeply committed to not just winning but dominating—as well embodied by 1927's starting lineup known as Murderer's Row. For now, Ruppert was just entering the business of professional sports, but he already appreciated the importance of proven talent—or at least its marquee value. Garrison was clearly on the downside of his career.

For all his success and talent on the track, Garrison's life on Sportsmen's Row—much like Jockey McLaughlin's—was far from harmonious. Garrison was something of a chronic gambler—not a high-stakes, deliberative professional (like Mike Dwyer) but rather more impulsive in nature. Though he might go from rich to poor in a matter of days, his successful career in the saddle inevitably ensured a steady income. As long as his riding stayed competitive, there'd always be another paycheck for him to gamble away. Garrison seemed to lose more than he won, however, and his personal and professional relationships repeatedly suffered.

Shortly after he moved to number 30, rumors began to circulate about troubles between the jockey and his father-in-law over the management of their racing operation.[53] The stable had not been performing well, and by the end of 1889 there was open disagreement about its direction. Though the two had tried to work out their differences, the issue shortly became a matter for the courts. On the last day of the year, Garrison filed a restraining order against his father-in-law, preventing him from writing checks from their business account and demanding access to the stable's financial records. Garrison also announced his intention of going to race in England that spring with the gambler "Pittsburgh" Phil.

On the first day of the New Year, Garrison arrived at the Clifton, New Jersey racetrack looking "as natty as ever."[54] As knowledge of the suit spread among the crowd, so did rumors that Garrison was in desperate financial straits. He was even said to have borrowed money just to get to the track. The jockey's appearance and demeanor suggested otherwise, and he gave no indication as to his fiscal health. It was certainly difficult *prima facie* to comprehend; Garrison's earnings were, after all, quite well known, and—as the *Brooklyn Daily Eagle* noted—"when he bought the elegant three story basement and brownstone house at 30 Eighth Avenue last spring he was believed to be a comparatively rich man."[55] The next day, several reporters descended on Sportsmen's Row to inquire after the gossip. A small servant boy met them at the door and relayed that the jockey "wouldn't say anything. He is not feeling well."[56]

It would get worse. A few days later, Garrison was also served with papers by his mother-in-law, Sarah F. McMahon, seeking to dissolve their three-year partnership (separate from that of her husband) in the buying and training of racehorses. In the suit, she claimed that they jointly owned fifteen horses worth some $20,000 but that Garrison's stake was no more than $6,000. In the course of adjudication, Mrs. McMahon retained as counsel one William J. Gaynor, whose brilliant legal career would eventually lead to the mayoralty of New York City—and who would also later purchase number 20 Eighth Avenue and take his place on Sportsmen's Row in 1894.

Both legal matters would be decided by the end of January 1890, with the courts ruling in favor of Mrs. McMahon and Judge McMahon. The McMahon & Co. Stable was liquidated and its horses subsequently sold at auction on April 7, 1890. Garrison, fresh paycheck in hand, attended the sale, purchasing the chestnut mare Speedwell but passing on his namesake Garrison, a brown colt.

Family and financial woes aside, Garrison's generally likable and gregarious nature helped ensure his popularity. It also seems to have deflected any undue scrutiny of his gambling. There had always been rumors, but nothing that warranted action; it also helped that the sport was generally unregulated until early 1891 and that gambling was both ubiquitous and central to its popularity. In June 1891, however, Garrison came under suspicion of having profited from a race by deliberately losing it.[57] The charge may have been spurious—and no evidence of malfeasance was ever found—but the years of gossip and rumor surrounding Garrison gave it some credibility. At the time, there was actually no regulation in this regard, so the Board of Control set about instituting one, immediately suspending Garrison's license. The punishment was severe (and quite unpopular), but the Board of Control meant business, and making Garrison an example was an effective demonstration of its resolve.

Garrison's license was reinstated in the early fall of 1891, and he managed to stay out of apparent trouble for the next few years. By the summer of 1896, however, financial troubles had reappeared. That August, the entire contents of number 30 were put up for auction, "by order of the owner, a shining young member of the turf."[58] The reason for the sale is unknown, but its urgency and comprehensiveness—literally the entire contents were cleared out, from Garrison's prized billiard table to the crockery and linens—suggest some measure of financial distress. Gambling may have indeed been a factor. Later that year, he was accused of running an illegal poolroom at the Putnam Pleasure Club (located at the corner of Downing and Fulton Streets).[59] The police investigated and, finding nothing more illicit than chess and checkers at the club, dropped the charges. By 1897, number 30 had been rented out, and Garrison had moved on.

Garrison's departure from Sportsmen's Row generally corresponds with the end of his racing career. For all of his talent, he—like many aging jockeys—constantly battled weight issues, which ultimately curtailed his time in the saddle, and a comeback in 1899 as a jumper was short-lived. Though the total number of races in which he competed and placed is unknown, Garrison himself later estimated that he had ridden in more than ten thousand races, won over seven hundred contests and collected more than $2 million in purses. Following his retirement, he remained active and popular in the sport, occupying himself variously as owner, trainer, starter and official. Given his charm, charisma and popularity, he also briefly tried his hand at acting.

Garrison Finish (1914), starring Sid Smith as Snapper Garrison. *Courtesy of www.rainfall.com.*

Garrison suffered a stroke and died of heart failure at Brooklyn's Swedish Hospital on October 28, 1930. He left an impressive legacy. His signature move—the come-from-behind Garrison Finish—ushered a sports idiom that remained popular for the next half century.[60] He was also the subject of a book, *Garrison's Finish: A Romance of the Race-course*, by W.B.M. Ferguson (1906) and two silent films (based on Ferguson's book), the first in 1914 and the second in 1923, starring Jack Pickford (Mary's brother). In 1955, he was also elected to the inaugural hall of fame class at the National Museum of Racing in Saratoga.

Due to his far-reaching celebrity, Garrison is the best remembered of the sportsmen and the most closely identified with Sportsmen's Row. Most recently, the jockey and his former home, number 30, were featured on the 2007 Park Slope Civic Council house tour.

JAMES ROWE, NUMBER 12 EIGHTH AVENUE

In contrast to Garrison, Rowe's time on Sportsmen's Row is something of a mystery. Although arguably the most significant in terms of renown and lasting legacy to the sport, he is the least remembered of the sportsmen associated with the block. Although he didn't sell number 12 until January 1897, after 1893 he was never again mentioned in the context of Sportsmen's Row. The April 19, 1896 *Brooklyn Daily Eagle*, for instance, ran a detailed article entitled "The Park Slope's Growth," which lists the Dwyer brothers ("the meteors of the racetrack"), McLaughlin and Garrison as the sportsmen associated with Sportsmen's Row, conspicuously failing to mention Rowe.

This apparent absence may have been a result of Rowe's peculiar career as a starter, of which even the basic chronology is unclear.[61] Rowe's transition to starter and early work with the flag were generally well received. By 1893, however, his performance was increasingly open to criticism. Some of the accusations were credible ("careless" when the heavily favored Clifford was left at the gate in the 1894 Brooklyn Handicap), others less so (such as "posing"). By 1895, the *Thoroughbred Record* felt it necessary to offer an apologia of sorts for his apparent struggles.[62] These, the *Record* opined, were of neither "method [nor] judgment" but rather that he was handicapped by his long and diverse career in the turf, which caused the jockeys "to respect him not."

James G. Rowe Sr. (left). *Courtesy of Keeneland-Cook.*

Regardless, the Jockey Club and the track owners respected him enough that work was never in short supply. The money was also good (about $100 for a day's work), and Rowe took on additional starting responsibilities at a number of tracks in the mid-1890s, including on the West Coast during the winter months. What is quite clear is that Rowe spent a good portion of his time away from number 12.

Ultimately, and generally corresponding with his departure from Sportsmen's Row, Rowe returned to training and developed twenty-three more champions—the most on record.[63] He passed away on August 29, 1929, and, like McLaughlin and Garrison, was elected to the inaugural class of the hall of fame at the National Museum of Racing. Rowe's son, James Jr., followed in his footsteps and also became a successful trainer. Born in 1889, he also spent part of the first decade of his life as a resident of Sportsmen's Row.

PHIL DWYER, NUMBER 8 EIGHTH AVENUE

When Garrison split from his father-in-law in the winter of 1889–90, he boasted of going to England to race on its tracks. It was empty bluster and probably little more than a diversion from the troubles with his in-laws. At the time, though, the British had salivated at the thought of eviscerating Garrison and "Pittsburg" Phil, as Americans had generally performed quite poorly across the pond. As the *Weekly Irish Times* had then counseled, "[Though] Pittsburgh Phil will make some of the English and French bookmakers weary of his continual success...Phil must remember that all Americans who have left their native shores and pastures have gone home broke or heavy losers."[64] Despite the risks, the temptation to compete in England was powerful—a virtual siren song that promised unmatched riches and glory.

In early 1895, Mike Dwyer and his new partner heeded this call and set off for England with $250,000 and a stable of elite Thoroughbreds. They intended to take England by storm and make a fortune on its tracks. The trip—just as the *Weekly Irish Times* had predicted of Garrison's aborted venture—was an unmitigated disaster. Dwyer returned home that fall having lost his horses, his fortune and what remained of his health. Croker had a bit more success. He continued competing in England, culminating in a first place finish at the 1907 Epsom Derby with Orby.

Though Mike Dwyer continued to dabble in horses, he had fallen far from the time when he was the "most active of all the horse lovers on the track, when the crowd followed him about and imitated on a small scale his plays, and when his judgment on a horse was final."[65] He died on August 19, 1906, in Gravesend, at his modest home near the racetrack that he had started with his brother just twenty years before.

In his last years, all of Mike's needs—expenses, full-time care, et cetera— were provided for by his brother, who remained prosperous to the last. Phil permanently departed Sportsmen's Row in 1901 but was there infrequently in the latter years of his residency.

Opposite, top: Mike Dwyer (seated). The man on the far right is Foxhall Keene, a prominent Thoroughbred owner and champion poloist. *Courtesy of Keeneland-Hemment.*

Opposite, bottom: Phil Dwyer (second from left). *Courtesy of Keeneland-Hemment.*

The Sportsmen, 1892–1900

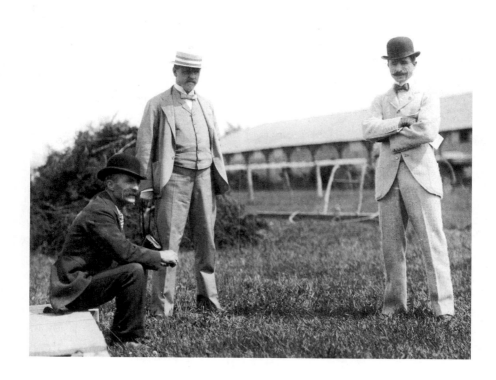

Phil had always been the savvier of the two brothers, and his business instincts had served him well. In 1904, in addition to his leadership of the Brooklyn Jockey Club, he became president of the Queens County Jockey Club and its Aqueduct track in Queens. It was here that he would ultimately leave his most enduring mark on the sport, establishing Aqueduct as one of the great (and profitable) regional tracks. Purchasing adjacent land, he expanded the complex, extending its track and rebuilding its stands. On the occasion of his sixty-fifth birthday on August 21, 1909, he was honored for his many contributions to the sport. The celebration was attended by many of his friends and former colleagues, including McLaughlin and Rowe.

On the morning of May 29, 1917, a seventy-two-year-old Dwyer was chauffeured to the Belmont racetrack to catch the running of the Metropolitan Handicap. It was a cold, damp and dreary day, and Phil returned home feeling unwell. He contracted pneumonia and died on June 9 at his home in Manhattan's Hotel Wolcott. He passed away, fittingly, just as the Suburban Handicap was ending at Belmont Park; it was the first running he had missed since the race's inception in 1884. His last words were reportedly an inquiry as to who had won the race.[66]

In death, Phil was reunited with his brother, sister-in-law and son in the Dwyer family plot in the Cemetery of the Holy Cross. Among those in attendance at the funeral was James Rowe. The racing magnate left an estate estimated at $1 million, which was subsequently distributed to his and Mike's surviving children. In tribute to the Dwyer brothers, the Brooklyn Derby, which the brothers established in 1887, was renamed the Dwyer Stakes in 1918.

SPORTSMEN'S ROW, TRANSCENDENT

A contemporary horse racing fan might have found it surprising that Rowe, Garrison and the Dwyers would have been neighbors. Rowe's split with the Dwyers in 1884 was generally believed to have been quite acerbic, and his working relationship with Garrison during their time together with Belmont was considered strained at best. Off the track, however, relations among the sportsmen appear to have been quite cordial. They shared a number of mutual interests, notably boxing, of which they attended a number of matches together. Accordingly, the benefits of living in proximity (convenience of travel, shared anxieties, access to opportunities, et cetera) might have outweighed any apparent disadvantages. This is further suggested by the fact that Garrison and Rowe had previously been neighbors on Sixth Avenue, Garrison at number 91 and Rowe at 73. The friendship among the sportsmen's wives may have also played a role, and that between Mrs. Dwyer and Mrs. McLaughlin likely influenced their husbands' original decision to purchase adjoining houses on Eighth Avenue. Furthermore, such a living arrangement was not entirely unique. Rowe and Daly later lived along a stretch of Avenue U known as "Trainer's Row." Located near the Sheepshead Bay racetrack, it counted among its residents such turf notables as W.B. Jennings, Frank Taylor, Tom Walsh, Jack Goldsborough, J.J. Hyland and Archie Zimmerman.[67]

Though the sportsmen's actual time as residents of Sportsmen's Row was relatively short—and the time that four of the five were all in residence together was even shorter—their association with northern Eighth Avenue is quite remarkable. While they all lived within a one-block stretch, by the mid-1890s the designation "Sportsmen's Row" had become generally associated with a broader expanse of Eighth Avenue. An attempted suicide in 1895 outside number 79 Eighth Avenue (between Union and President Streets, some two blocks south) was notably identified, for instance, as occurring on Sportsmen's Row.[68]

Regardless of its actual veracity, the appellation Sportsmen's Row would have held undoubted appeal to the other residents of the block. McLaughlin, Garrison, Rowe and the Dwyer brothers were the indisputable sports icons of the age. They engaged in a sport that was extraordinarily popular and also one in which many of their wealthy and politically connected neighbors took more than just a passing interest; so much so, in fact, that the concept and cachet of Sportsmen's Row would credibly transcend even that of its eponymous sportsmen.

THE BROOKLYN JOCKEY CLUB

A Neighborhood Affair

When Phil and Mike Dwyer set out to build their own racetrack, they aimed their sights on a location perfectly suited for their venture: the old Prospect Park Fairgrounds in the town of Gravesend. The topography and soil of the area were ideal, and it was inexpensively and well serviced by public transportation. It had also played host to horse racing for almost twenty years. In 1868, it had become home to the Prospect Park Ground and Race Course, which was well known in the 1870s for its popular trotting track.

The park was also situated near Brooklyn's two existing Thoroughbred racetracks. The Brighton Beach course, which opened on June 28, 1879, was located between Ocean Parkway and Coney Island Avenue to the east and west and Sheepshead Bay Road and Sea Breeze Avenue to the north and south. It was operated by the Brighton Beach Racing Association and had a decidedly proletarian demeanor. Its purses were lower, and it attracted a tough, working-class crowd. The Sheepshead Bay track, on the other hand, was considerably more refined. Nicknamed the "American Ascot," its clubhouse Gold Room regularly attracted the nation's wealthiest and most prominent turf aficionados. It was inaugurated on June 19, 1880, and operated by the Coney Island Jockey Club, whose founders included August Belmont, Pierre Lorillard Jr. and Leonard Jerome, father of Jenny Jerome, the mother of Sir Winston Churchill. It was located on a 125-acre plot bordered by Ocean Avenue and Haring Street (to the east and west) and Avenues V and X (to the north and south). Among its major races were the

Suburban, Realization and Futurity, which—with its $40,900 purse—was the most lucrative stakes in the country.

The Dwyer brothers acquired the Prospect Park Fairgrounds in early 1886. At the time, the grounds contained a serviceable track and a number of structures in varying states of disrepair; though the Coney Island Jockey Club had leased the complex for its 1879 inaugural season, much of the facility, including its grandstand, was destroyed by fire in 1884. The Dwyers undertook a rapid overhaul and expansion of the site, and the new Gravesend racetrack was completed in the late summer of 1886.[69] The grounds occupied some sixty acres between Ocean Parkway and Gravesend (now McDonald) Avenue (to the east and west, respectively) and Kings Highway and Avenue U (to the north and south). The track, which was one mile long, was 128 feet wide at its starting post and could accommodate thirty horses. The straightaways were 80 feet wide and the banked turns 100 feet in width.

The monumental grandstand was 400 feet long, some 128 feet longer than the one at Sheepshead Bay. It was two stories tall and made of yellow Georgia pine set on a brick foundation. The first floor contained a restaurant with adjoining bar, lavatories and icehouse, while that above held a seating gallery that could accommodate eight thousand spectators. Offices and the jockeys' weighing-in and locker room were located adjacent to the restaurant. To the immediate south of the grandstand were the mounting paddocks and a small, private clubhouse. North of the grandstand was a betting pavilion, which could hold up to one hundred bookmakers, and a large carriage shed with storage for several hundred vehicles on race days.

On the opposite side of the track, between the backstretch and Coney Island Avenue, were the stables and main clubhouse, the latter being one of the few surviving buildings from the original Prospect Park Ground and Race Course. The Prospect Park and Coney Island Railroad (PP&CI), which ran along Gravesend Avenue, built a spur onto the racetrack grounds that discharged patrons at the grandstand; the stop was simply called "Race Track." The PP&CI was the antecedent of the modern F train, whose route it still follows. The F is even now on occasion referred to as the "Culver Line" after the railroad's founder, Andrew Culver.

The racetrack was managed by the Brooklyn Jockey Club, which was incorporated in March 1886 with a capital stock of $500,000. Five thousand shares were issued and split among its nine directors, who included Mike Dwyer and a number of nationally prominent racing men. Phil Dwyer

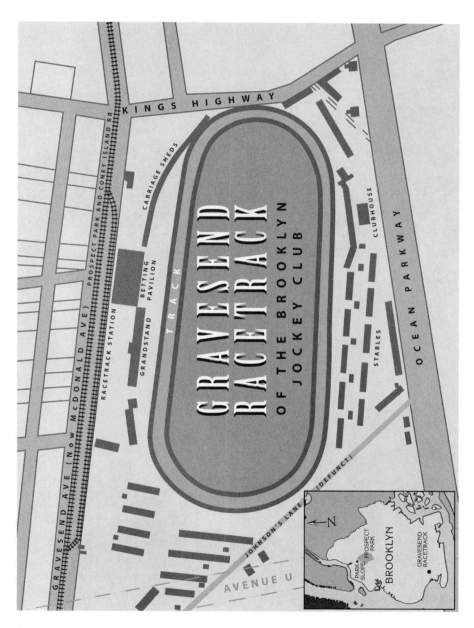

Plan of the Brooklyn Jockey Club's Gravesend racetrack.

Grandstand, starter's platform and track of the Brooklyn Jockey Club's Gravesend racetrack. *Courtesy of Brown Brothers.*

Grandstand of the Brooklyn Jockey Club's Gravesend racetrack. *Courtesy of Brown Brothers.*

assumed the club's presidency, and the club adopted the colors of the Dwyer Stable (red and blue) in its flags, bunting and decorations.

OPENING DAY

The Gravesend Racetrack opened to the public on August 26, 1886.[70] Many notable patrons of the turf were in attendance, including several leading members of the Coney Island and Brighton Beach racing associations, particularly Leonard Jerome. The day was hot and dry, and some twenty thousand boisterous spectators crammed the grandstand and viewing lawns. At 2:00 p.m. sharp, the inaugural race of the Brooklyn Jockey Club was run, and its winner, appropriately, was Snapper Garrison riding Little Minch. The purse netted $750, and both horse and jockey were awarded elaborate floral wreaths to mark the occasion. Garrison went on to win the next two races, as well as a $500 bet from Jockey McLaughlin, whom he defeated in the third contest. The final race had concluded by 5:30 p.m., though much of the crowd lingered long afterward in celebration of the club's opening day. It was, by every measure, a terrific success.

For all of its hasty organization and implementation, the Brooklyn Jockey Club had in fact been quite masterfully conceived. The sport was entering the height of its popularity, and its local fan base was more than sufficient to support three Thoroughbred tracks. Moreover, the club catered to an audience that occupied the middle ground between the lowbrow Brighton Beach and high-end Sheepshead Bay organizations. Though its facility was the smallest of the three, it was better located than Brighton and assured of more steady patronage. This was important as gate receipts—i.e. tickets, concessions, parking, et cetera—were an important part of the sport's earnings and had been since about 1829. In time, "gate" would comprise the fundamental revenue stream for all professional sports. For now, it was just one of the many precedents that horse racing would bequeath to the modern business of sports.

To eliminate head-to-head competition and maximize attendance, the Brooklyn Jockey Club also scheduled its races on the off days of the Coney Island Jockey Club. As a result, there were now races held every day in Brooklyn during the season (roughly mid-May to early

October). Coney Island ran on Tuesdays, Thursdays and Saturdays, while Brooklyn took to the turf on Monday, Wednesdays and Fridays. In later years, the three clubs would further divide up the racing season for mutual benefit.

The club also established (and funded) several key races, notably the Brooklyn Derby, Gazelle, Great American, Tremont and Expectation. The Brooklyn Handicap, first run in the club's second year (1887), soon became one of the great classics, rivaling—if not exceeding—that of the Suburban; of note, six horses later trained by James Rowe would go on to take its laurels. As far as patronage and quality of competition, the club was an immediate success, and by 1888 it was financially profitable as well. The Dwyers' place in the pantheon of horse racing titans was all but ensured.

Back on Eighth Avenue, the club's success would also accrue to many of its other residents: that Sportsmen's Row could be a reasonable synecdoche for northern Eighth Avenue had much to do with the fact that many of its inhabitants, in addition to McLaughlin, the Dwyer brothers, Garrison and Rowe, also maintained an active interest in and association with the sport and specifically with the Brooklyn Jockey Club. In many ways, the club was the unifying theme around which the identity of Sportsmen's Row ultimately coalesced.

ROBERT PINKERTON, NUMBERS 39 AND 71 EIGHTH AVENUE

On the opening day of the Gravesend racetrack, security was provided by the Pinkerton Detective Agency. Company principal Robert Pinkerton (b. December 12, 1848) personally oversaw the operations, working to ensure that the club's inaugural race card was a success. He was head of the agency's East Coast operation, a position he had assumed following the death of his father (and company founder), Allan Pinkerton. His brother William, headquartered in Chicago, oversaw the western operation.

Allan Pinkerton (August 25, 1819–July 1, 1884) established the Pinkerton Detective Agency shortly after the Civil War, having gained much experience managing President Lincoln's security detail and heading up the United States Secret Service. The company quickly

Robert Pinkerton (left) at an unidentified racetrack. *Courtesy of Keeneland-Cook.*

became known for its professionalism, scrupulous attention to detail and success in crime fighting and prevention. It was the first organization of its type to collect information on suspects (such as taking mug shots), and its company motto ("We never sleep") and logo (an eye) gave rise to the expression "private eye." Significantly, all Pinkerton agents were bound to a code that required upright living and adherence to a set of principles (such as accept no bribes). In the decades following the war, the agency expanded its operations, providing direct support (particularly union busting) to a variety of industries. In this capacity, it developed an early relationship with horse racing, offering a range of services and experienced personnel (such as guards, gatekeepers and ushers) to the various national jockey clubs.[71] It was critical to the operational success of the Brooklyn Jockey Club.

Pinkerton security would also become indispensable in the spring of 1891, when the club became embroiled in a war with the illegal but extraordinarily popular off-track betting parlors and their agents.[72] Gambling was (and is) central to horse racing.[73] Though more or less legal in New York State since

1830, it was a frequent target of self-styled moral crusaders and organizations such as the Society for the Prevention of Crime, which repeatedly challenged its existence on both legal and moral grounds. Though threatened, the popularity of the sport (and its political connections) generally thwarted any efforts to effect an outright ban. At the same time, some distinction was made between those who gambled at the track and those who did so off the track. While the latter were interested exclusively in gambling, the former were seen as at least supporting the sport (by paying admission to its tracks). And so, in 1887, New York State passed the Ives Pool Law, which placed restrictions on gambling while also collecting revenue for its toleration. Bookmaking was confined to officially sanctioned tracks, and the state received 5 percent of the gross gate receipts.

The off-track poolrooms generally remained open, though operated at somewhat greater discretion. They remained popular among the lower and working classes who were otherwise unable to travel to (or priced out of) the track. To effectively conduct their business, however, the poolrooms required real-time race information (such as jockey selections, weights, scratches and especially race results), which the Ives Pool Law effectively contravened. The racetracks themselves were also keen to eliminate off-track betting, which presented direct competition that siphoned away potential customers and money. Still, the poolrooms found their way to the information, generally abetted by the Western Union Telegraph Company, which found the association lucrative and whose transmission wires provided some cover in the form of legitimate racetrack news.

At the opening of the 1891 racing season, Phil Dwyer drew a line in the sand. He closed the Union Telegraph office and ordered the Pinkertons to prevent any race information from leaving the track. What unfolded that season was an increasingly bizarre struggle to stem the tide of race information that pitted the club and the Pinkertons against the Poolsellers' Association and Western Union. At the start of the season, fans leaving early (with racing information in hand) led Dwyer to seal the gates for the duration of a race card. The negative publicity was damning, so Dwyer rescinded the order but had early departures escorted through a far gate away from any posted information. Next, "spectators" appeared who communicated by gesture to spotters outside the track, who in turn telegraphed the information to the poolrooms. Dwyer responded by putting up a 50-foot wall around the track. Union Telegraph then erected a 120-foot tower to peer inside. Thereafter, it was tossed balls, semaphores and even carrier pigeons hidden under ladies' hoop dresses. The Pinkertons fought back with brute force and a campaign of misinformation, capturing and releasing the pigeons with erroneous intelligence. At one point, the club even employed Snapper Garrison—during his brief suspension for gambling that season—to shoot the pigeons as they left the track. He was apparently also a crack shot. It made for a wild racing season, with the action in the stands exceeding that on the track—and the club ultimately realizing its highest gate receipts to date.

By the end of the summer, the poolrooms seemed to have finally gained the upper hand, devising their most ingenious stratagem yet: a party of spectators who came to the races in their elegant barouche, setting up on a small hill above the betting pavilion. They went about their activities in a most inconspicuous fashion, enjoying the races with food, wine and cigars. They occasionally mingled with their driver, who sat on the coach in his tall hat. In an uproarious crowd, their seemingly innocuous actions were, in fact, deeply choreographed. Each member was collecting information and reporting back to the driver, who relayed the information with his foot via a telegraph in the carriage floor and transmitted by means of an electric light on the top of his hat. The light was invisible to anyone on the grounds but visible to a nearby spotter. After six days, the artifice was betrayed, and it was Robert Pinkerton who personally stormed the barouche and seized the driver (an electrician paid $1,000 a day for his work).

Pinkerton had become deeply engaged and committed to his work with the club, and he had grown close to the Dwyers in the process. He had also become their neighbor, moving to number 39 Eighth Avenue in 1889.[74] Unlike his turf associates, Pinkerton played an immediate and substantial role in local society; his profession garnered him significant respect and always made for interesting dinner conversation. His daughter Anna was enrolled in the exclusive Packer Institute and was soon considered one of the most popular (and eligible) girls in the neighborhood. A party held for her in February 1892 in number 39 brought out all of Brooklyn's ranking matrons and their daughters.[75] The theme was "pink," and the house was adorned accordingly. The front and back parlors were festooned with pink roses and palms, while six dining tables decorated with pink tablecloths and ribbons were arranged around the parlor.

By the mid-1890s, Pinkerton had outgrown number 39 and set his eyes on a property a little farther south: the newly built number 71 Eighth Avenue, at the intersection of Union Street. Erected by William Flanagan—who had

Number 39 Eighth Avenue, a stunning French neo-Grec town house built in 1882. Note the wide stoop and imposing entrance portico.

previously constructed numbers 20–26 Eighth Avenue in 1883—the four-story limestone town house is an outstanding example of the Neoclassical style of the period.[76] It was situated in a prime location, directly opposite the palatial house of M.V. Phillips (built 1887) and diagonally across from the mansion of J. Rogers Maxwell (demolished in 1922). The Pinkertons moved in 1895 and celebrated with a lavish house-warming party. Number 71's opulent parlor also played host to the reception following Anna's marriage on November 14, 1900, considered one of the notable social events of the season.[77]

Pinkerton's time on Eighth Avenue was not entirely without controversy.[78] A little before 3:00 a.m. on April 10, 1904, a patrolman was making his nightly rounds when he passed by a stable at 782 Union Street. He heard cheering from within and summoned backup from his Bergen Street precinct to investigate. When the police entered the premises, they came upon a cockfight with some fifty men watching a black cock take on a Spanish red. In the ensuing chaos, about a dozen of the spectators escaped, though the police managed to take thirty-two men and twenty-five gamecocks into custody. The police subsequently marched the detainees to the precinct house in full view of the surrounding residents, who had come to their windows on account of all the noise and commotion.

The next day, after it came to light that 782 Union Street belonged to Robert Pinkerton, newspaper reporters descended upon number 71 for comment. Pinkerton was away on the West Coast, but his wife claimed ignorance and surprise at the whole sordid affair. As it turned out, those arrested at Pinkerton's stable composed the cream of local society or, at the very least, their sons. All were united by their "sporting proclivities" and had apparently been engaged in cockfighting for some time. The raid became the talk of the town and set tongues wagging as to who would be formally named. To make matters worse, the Society for the Prevention of Cruelty to Animals committed itself to lobbying for the public exposure and maximum punishment of those convicted. Of particular interest was the identity of one "Alan Budd," who had been separated from the other prisoners at the police station. The rumor was that Alan Budd was, in fact, Allan Pinkerton, Robert's son. In the end—and over the strenuous objection of the SPCA and the prosecution—twenty-nine of those charged received the minimum sentence, a $10 fine, while two others were fined $100. "Alan Budd" appeared in person—a fashionably dressed, if nervous, young man—and was ordered to pay $10. Few of

Number 71 Eighth Avenue.

those presented before the court were believed to have used their real names, and some were likely ringers. The Alan Budd who presented himself was not Allan Pinkerton, nor could he be identified by any of the newspapers. The whole matter was largely swept away, and those involved retained their anonymity. Pinkerton's stable at 782 Union Street, on the other hand, would go on to play a major role in the later history of Park Slope. It is now part of the Park Slope Food Coop (PSFC), a progressive neighborhood institution founded in 1973. The PSFC is presently one of the largest such cooperative organizations; in the fiscal year ending in 2010, it rang up sales of $39.4 million.[79]

On August 12, 1907, Robert Pinkerton died of heart failure aboard a passenger steamer while en route to Europe.[80] He left an estate worth $3 million and a portfolio of real estate holdings, including 71 Eighth Avenue and 782 Union Street, to his wife. Oversight of the Pinkerton Detective Agency fell to his brother William, upon whose death in 1923 it passed to Robert's son Allan. Allan in turn passed away on October 7, 1930, notably leaving $1,000 to Snapper Garrison (who would also die later that same month).[81] The Pinkerton home at 71 Eighth Avenue would remain in the possession of the family until the passing of Robert Pinkerton's widow, Anne, on November 21, 1933.[82]

RICHARD HYDE, NUMBER 22 EIGHTH AVENUE

Richard Hyde, who lived at number 22 Eighth Avenue, was—along with his business partner, Louis Behman—the largest investor in the Brooklyn Jockey Club.[83] The partners had financed the acquisition of the Gravesend racetrack grounds, including the original Prospect Park Fairgrounds and adjoining lots. They conveyed a half interest in these to the Dwyers in exchange for seats on the club's board of directors and a good number of its ownership shares. Their involvement with the club was extensive and their working relationship with the Dwyer brothers rather substantial. In their own right, they were also quite distinguished.

Hyde (b. May 22, 1849) and Behman (b. June 4, 1855) were two of the most important theater impresarios of the age.[84] Having first met as schoolmates at Brooklyn's P.S. 1, circumstance later brought them together again at the 1876 Philadelphia Centennial. It was there that they partnered to open

Richard Hyde.

their first musical theater, followed by another in Baltimore a year later. Returning to Brooklyn, they opened a string of theaters and subsequently others in New York City, Newark, Pittsburg and Chicago. They specialized in vaudeville, burlesque and variety acts, which they also disseminated via a series of successful touring companies. Their flagship Brooklyn theatre was located on Adams Street and opened as the Brooklyn Volks Garden in May 1877. When this burned to the ground on June 10, 1890, the partners rebuilt the theater at an out-of-pocket cost of some $125,000. Renamed Hyde & Behman's, it had a seating capacity of 1,800 and soon became one of the most popular and financially successful stages in the city. In sum, the partners were enterprising, entrepreneurial and quite rich. They had also made their fortune in public entertainment, of which the spectator sport of horse racing was a logical cognate.

Hyde had moved to the newly built number 22 Eighth Avenue in 1884, at the same time that Mike Dwyer and James McLaughlin had made numbers 26 and 24 their homes. It was a sensible choice, permitting Hyde easy access to his theaters and the downtown business district. With the formation of the Brooklyn Jockey Club, proximity to his new business partners offered additional benefits—as did accessibility to the Gravesend track. Although Hyde's financial backing was central to the venture's success, he was, by and large, a silent partner, generally assenting to Phil Dwyer's leadership and day-to-day oversight of the club.

Nevertheless, Hyde was still closely identified with the operation. In 1888, a new rail line was proposed for Ocean Parkway that would run alongside the Gravesend track. It met with fierce opposition, in part because of its potential despoilment of the beautiful tree-lined boulevard. As William Osborn, an angry letter writer to the *Brooklyn Daily Eagle*, put it:[85] "Ocean Parkway is one of the grandest drives in the world, and every year, as the trees grow larger, its appearance will become more magnificent. Straight to the ocean, it is a drive of which no other city can boast."[86] And in closing, he added, "If Mr. Hyde, of Messrs Hyde and Behman, wishes to facilitate travel to his race track on the days of races let him put omnibuses out as great dry goods houses do for the benefit of the patrons."

Two days later, Hyde responded in the same paper:

> *Why Mr. Osborne should connect me with it, or where he gets his information from that I desire such a road to be constructed, I am at a loss to imagine. When he refers to the Brooklyn Jockey Club racetrack as my racetrack he must either be endeavoring to poke fun at me or else somebody*

Hyde & Behman's flagship theater was located on Adams Street in downtown Brooklyn. *Courtesy of the Brooklyn Public Library, Brooklyn Collection.*

must be endeavoring to "string" him. It would appear, therefore, that Mr. Osborne's criticisms were based entirely upon an imaginary predicate.

The racetrack, of course, was very much his, even if the accusation was ultimately without merit (and there seems to have been no other connection between Hyde and Osborne). In the end, the line was never built, and Ocean Parkway was spared any untoward violation.

Beyond number 22, northern Eighth Avenue proved alluring to Hyde's entrepreneurial impulse in other ways. In January 1893, he and Behman purchased the apartment building on the southeast corner of Eighth Avenue and Plaza Street, on the east side of Sportsmen's Row (just opposite the recently completed 8 and 10 Eighth Avenue). On the occasion, the *Brooklyn Daily Eagle* offered a description of Sportsmen's Row with its full array of sportsmen in residence:[87]

> *The property is opposite what is known as Sportsmen's Row. Michael and Philip Dwyer, the millionaire horsemen occupying houses on the corner of Lincoln and St. John's places, and ex-Mayor Chapin, Richard Hyde of Hyde & Behman, James Rowe, the trainer and starter, Percy G. Williams and Robert A. Furey owning houses in the row, and Snapper Garrison, the jockey, on the adjoining block. The Montauk club is on the opposite end of the block to this site, and Mr. Chapin owns the intervening lots. It is one of the finest locations in the city, being on the crown of the hill, opposite the park and Soldiers and Sailors monument. The price paid is between $50,000 and $60,000.*

The apartment building Hyde and Behman purchased actually consisted of two adjoining four-story stone and brick structures, which the partners intended to demolish and replace with a "family" hotel. Though they went as far as to hire an architect (Peter J. Lauritzen, who had designed the Union League Club on Bedford Avenue), their hotel—for reasons unknown—was never realized. It is possible that some opposition was afforded by the other residents of the row, whose opinions Hyde was duty bound to respect. The adjacent plot of land owned by Chapin, however, would later play a central role in the history of Sportsmen's Row. For now, its open space served to provide the residents of Sportsmen's Row an unobstructed view onto Grand Army Plaza and the park beyond, a vista that added to the desirability of the block.

PERCY G. WILLIAMS, NUMBER 20 EIGHTH AVENUE

When the *Eagle* made note of Hyde and Behman's 1893 purchase, it mentioned Percy G. Williams as one of Sportsmen's Row's notable residents. Hyde was actually not the only theater magnate living on the block at the time; his neighbor Williams was also on his way to becoming one of the leading national figures of theater, particularly vaudeville.[88]

Percy Williams was born in Baltimore in 1857, the son of an eminent doctor. He initially pursued a career in medicine but soon dropped out of school to become an actor. He met some initial success on the stage, notably performing in a well-received traveling production of *Uncle Tom's Cabin*. In the 1880s, he settled in Brooklyn and gave up the stage. He did, however, put his acting skills to good use, selling dubious medical cures cooked up by his father. It proved financially lucrative, and Williams subsequently expanded his entrepreneurial portfolio to include real estate development.

In 1889, Williams moved to number 20 Eighth Avenue, which had been vacant for much of the year following the death of its previous owner, Frank Bassett (whose granddaughter had been at the center of some terrifically salacious gossip after a mysterious accident befell her estranged husband).[89] At the time, Williams was working with Thomas Adams Jr. (he of chewing gum fame who resided at 115 Eighth Avenue) on developing the area of Bergen Beach, three hundred acres of swampland in outer Brooklyn. They originally intended to build housing, but with the success of Coney Island opted to construct an amusement park instead. Their finished resort offered a range of amenities, including baths, restaurants and a boardwalk. It also had a casino, which at the time simply meant a place for entertainment. It was here that Williams reengaged his love of the theater, producing a number of successful musicals.

Williams spent a good portion of his time at the Bergen Beach casino, indulging his thespian fancy. And so, like many men of means, he employed a private guard to look after number 20 while he was away.[90] Williams's watchman was one Adolph Berg (who resided at number 17 Sterling Place), whose day job was special officer of the Brooklyn District Telegraph Company. Berg, however, was also a thief and had been pilfering various items from the houses he had been employed to watch. The police had their suspicions about him for some time—he had once been caught almost red-handed but talked his way out of the potential imbroglio—but nothing

Percy Williams. *Courtesy of the Brooklyn Public Library, Brooklyn Collection.*

definitive. On the afternoon of October 24, 1891, a detective from the local precinct happened to be looking for stolen goods at a pawnshop in New York City when in walked Berg seeking to barter some items. Upon returning to his precinct house, the officer was informed that Williams's house had been robbed that afternoon. The detective quickly deduced that Berg was the culprit and set out to arrest him. On his way to Berg's home, he ran into the suspect on Flatbush Avenue; in a bundle under Berg's arm were the stolen objects. Berg first tried to claim it was a simple misunderstanding and that he was on his way to Williams's house to return the objects. Under interrogation, however, he confessed to the theft but denied responsibility for any of the others of which he was suspected. A subsequent search of his belongings produced a skeleton key, which had provided him with unfettered access to number 20.

Number 20 was undoubtedly a tempting target for Berg. It was well appointed, as befit a man who was successful in business and a rising star in the arts. Williams was socially active and belonged to several important clubs (including the Amaranth Dramatic Association), and his son attended the newly chartered St. Paul's School in Garden City, Long Island, whose mission was to "develop manly, Christian character, a strong physique, and the power to think."[91] Behind number 20's mahogany door, however, Williams spent much of his time drinking himself into a stupor, a habit to which his son apparently also aspired while at St. Paul's. He and several schoolmates were expelled in May 1894 for their second alcohol violation, having returned after a night of debauchery, "worse for their pleasure."[92]

In June 1894, Williams put number 20 and its luxury contents up for sale.[93] Among its notable furnishings were a Phelps & Son rosewood piano, a number of important oil paintings (including works by Auguste Toulmouche, Jean-Baptiste-Camille Corot and Alfred Thompson Bricher), several Wilton and Axminster Carpets and a large amount of high-quality furniture (such as an imported mahogany and gold Empire table). Williams had decided to sell the house and devote himself entirely to the theater, this time as a manager and owner.

Following his departure from Eighth Avenue, Williams would go on to build a vast portfolio of theaters, acquiring his first major property, East New York's Brooklyn Music Hall, in 1897. He would open his most famous and lucrative theater, the Orpheum (at 578 Fulton Street), on December 31, 1900. By 1905, Williams was one of the most important and respected figures in popular theater; performers in particular appreciated his high pay and favorable working conditions. He would later sell his vast holdings to the industry-leading B.F. Keith Vaudeville Circuit for $5.25 million. On July 21, 1923, Williams died of cirrhosis at his vast Pineacres estate in East Islip, New York. After his death, the forty-eight-acre grounds and its Tudor-style mansion became the Percy Williams Home for Aged Actors, which was shuttered in 1973.

WILLIAM J. GAYNOR, NUMBER 20 EIGHTH AVENUE

In late May 1894, Phil Dwyer was arrested and hauled before the court under the charge of promoting a lottery or, more accurately, that the running of the Brooklyn Handicap constituted a lottery. The charge was peculiar, but it was actually another salvo in the ongoing struggle between the tracks and the poolrooms. The accuser was Peter De Lacy, one of the richest and most powerful poolroom sellers and Phil Dwyer's sworn enemy. In the previous year, the Saxton Poolroom Bill had eliminated many of the legal loopholes that the poolrooms had used to stay in business, and De Lacy—his business hurting—was out for revenge.

The judge before whom Dwyer was presented was none other than William Gaynor,[94] who had previously tangled with Snapper Garrison during the 1890 dissolution of the McMahon & Co. stable. Gaynor's ruling on the matter would presage two themes that would dominate his later political thinking: the use of force to impose morals and the protection of individual liberties:[95]

[The Brooklyn Handicap] *is not a lottery, either in common speech, or within legal definition. A lottery depends on lot or chance, such as the casting of lots, the throwing of dice, or the turning of a wheel. In the scheme of this race, horse owners do not pay a sum to win a larger sum by lot or chance, but in order to enter into the contest of skill, endurance, and speed, upon which the stake depends. With the matter as a debatable moral question, I have nothing to do. I cannot make laws. I am bound to administer the laws as I find them...Racing horses for stakes may be bad, but unlawful arrests are worse. The arrest and detention of the defendant was unwarranted. It was an exercise of arbitrary power, and history teaches that we have more to fear from arbitrary power than from all species of gambling combined.*

The ruling was essentially fair and well reasoned, and Dwyer was discharged. Gaynor, however, was not exactly a stranger to the big races[96]—he notably held a mortgage on the Brighton racetrack—and a little over a month later, he would purchase number 20 Eighth Avenue from Percy Williams for $23,000, becoming Dwyer's neighbor on Sportsmen's Row.[97] Though curious, the move seems to have been entirely coincidental and garnered no mention by an otherwise gossip-hungry press. Later, however, his involvement with the sport would come back to haunt him. Gaynor's presence, in turn, would come to increasingly define the next two decades of Sportsmen's Row.

JAMES SHEVLIN, NUMBER 51 EIGHTH AVENUE

Gaynor took up residence on a block defined by the sportsmen and a number of important Democratic politicians. Ostensible differences aside, the two groups were actually quite closely associated. As the *Brooklyn Daily Eagle* remarked at the opening of the 1888 spring racing season at Gravesend:[98]

> *The Spring Meeting of the Brooklyn Jockey Club appears to be invested with as much interest for politicians as the opening of a political campaign. Each day's racing has been attended by large crowds of politicians, of grades ranging from ward heeler up to "leaders." On Thursday the attendance of politicians was so numerous as to evoke this comment from one of the spectators: "If Alderman McCarty should go into the judges' stand and call the roll of the Kings County Democratic General Committee I have no doubt that he would find a quorum present." Several managers of the club are popular politicians, and this fact may have something to do with the popularity of the track among politicians...*

Notable among these politicians was James Shevlin, the "first lieutenant of the old Democratic machine."[99] Born in Ireland in 1842, Shevlin came to Brooklyn with his widowed mother and two brothers when just a boy.[100] After service in the Union Navy during the Civil War—in which he barely survived an encounter with the Confederate ironclad *Merrimac*, escaping through a porthole from the sinking *Cumberland*—he entered politics. He

From the left: James Shevlin, William Gaynor and William Jennings Bryan. *Courtesy of the Library of Congress, Prints & Photographs Division, LC-DIG-ggbain-00079.*

soon came to the attention of Hugh McLaughlin, the powerful Democratic leader (and friend of Mike Dwyer). As McLaughlin's lieutenant, Shevlin's success was obtained through various political appointments, ranging from battalion chief in the Brooklyn Fire Department to warden of the Kings County Penitentiary.

Shevlin was also deeply involved in horse racing, where his political connections were quite useful, and he was one of the directors of the Brooklyn Jockey Club. In February 1896, he would purchase 51 Eighth Avenue (at the corner of Berkeley Place) for $26,000 in order to be "as near Sportsmen's Row as possible."[101] Subsequently, his involvement in horse racing would become even more significant, and he would assume directorships of both the Belmont Park and Saratoga Racing Associations. After Phil Dwyer's death in 1917, he would also succeed him as president of the Queens County Jockey Club. On November 24, 1924, Shevlin passed away at his home at 69 Eighth Avenue (next door to the Pinkertons), where he had moved several years before. In honor of his long service to the sport, the Shevlin Stakes were inaugurated at Aqueduct and run almost yearly until 1959.

MIRABEAU TOWNS, NUMBER 24 EIGHTH AVENUE

Mayor Chapin was one of the first and most consequential of the Democratic politicians to move to Eighth Avenue, and his career was also among the most productive.[102] He left the mayor's office in 1891, after which he served a brief term in Congress (November 1891–November 1892) and then worked for New York State as a railroad commissioner. Though he spent a good deal of his time away from number 24, he added several thousands of dollars in improvements and upgrades to the house. In early 1894, he put the brownstone—still "considered one of the most eligible properties on the Prospect Park Slope"—on the market for $35,000.[103] That March, after several days of haggling, he offered up the house to the lawyer Mirabeau Towns for significantly less: $15,000 in cash and Towns's Quincy Street home, valued at $10,000. Chapin later moved to Manhattan, where he returned to practicing law. He died on a trip to Canada on October 2, 1936, at the age of eighty-eight. His grandson, Hamilton Fish Jr. (aka IV), would also become a twelve-term New York congressmen—but on the other side of the aisle.

Number 24's new owner, Mirabeau Lamar Towns, was one of the most colorful residents of Sportsmen's Row.[104] Born in Alabama in 1852 to a successful family with deep southern roots, he was sent to Berlin to study at the Frederick William Gymnasium and thereafter at Tubingen University, where he received a doctorate in law. He returned to Georgia at twenty-one, cultured, a polyglot and deeply influenced by European thinking. Finding the South no longer appealing, he moved north and continued his study of the law at New York University. In 1876, he settled in Brooklyn, where he joined an established German lawyer in practice.

In the same year that he moved to Eighth Avenue, Towns was appointed a delegate to the Constitutional Convention. Though he had previously demonstrated some political acumen, it was here that he distinguished himself with his formidable oratorical and debating skills. Pursuit of political office, however, was almost entirely out of the question. His leanings were—in the opinion of *Harper's Weekly*—so "radical as to verge on socialism."[105] He was an early supporter of women's rights (where he established a number of legal precedents, including that a woman could sue and recover damages from another woman for alienation of her husband's affections), as well as for stricter regulation of industry and finance. Though smart and well respected, he was a man far ahead of his time—and totally unelectable.

He was also rather eccentric. Known as the "poet-lawyer," he was fond of addressing the court in verse, often grafting rhetorically complex statements on more pedestrian matters. In defending a woman from foreclosure in 1899—in which he argued, *inter alia*, that the terms of her mortgage were usurious—he channeled Alfred Lord Tennyson's "The Charge of the Light Brigade":[106]

Into the cashier's den
Rode the six hundred
To pay what they owed
Swift to be plundered
Earth had not known such men,
Free, open-handed;
Paying two thousand times
What was demanded.

His wife, Christine, also shared his idiosyncrasies. A philanthropist, she took special interest in the needs of children, if in somewhat peculiar ways. In 1910, this included distributing twenty thousand toy houses made of cement to the poor children of the city.[107]

By the time of his move, Towns had become a close confidant of William Gaynor.[108] He was also—like Gaynor and so many of their Democratic colleagues—a horse racing enthusiast and was often seen at the Brooklyn tracks.[109]

OTHER HORSE RACING NOTABLES

Robert Furey—whose contracting work had previously facilitated the marriage of Phil Dwyer's daughter—was not only the horse racing magnate's neighbor in number 10 but also an aficionado of the turf; a "veteran horseman," according to the *Brooklyn Daily Eagle*.[110] He was a regular at the racetracks and well known for his betting prowess; again, in the words of the *Eagle*, "Robert Furey has the reputation of a heavy bettor, but he seldom exhibits any bookmakers' tickets. He generally comes out of the racing season considerably ahead of the game." He was also counted among Mike Dwyer's close friends and was frequently in the social company of both brothers.[111] He had also (as was apparently something of an unofficial requirement for the residents of Sportsmen's Row) faced Gaynor in court several times, when the latter was counsel for the town of Gravesend. Once when the town owed $1,650 to Furey for road work and again during a long ownership squabble over Coney Island Point, a lucrative parcel of land in Gravesend.[112]

Next door in number 8, in addition to Phil Dwyer, several family members also pursued professional interests in horse racing: Phil Dwyer's son in the Dwyer & Son stable (1890–1893) and later his son-in-law, Joseph McGarry, beginning in 1900. An honorable mention must also be given to James Rowe Jr. in number 12. Though only a toddler at the time, he too would go on to establish his own legacy in the sport.

WILLIAM A. ENGEMAN, NUMBER 44 SEVENTH AVENUE

William A. Engeman, the head of the Brighton Beach Racing Association, lived one block west of Sportsmen's Row, at the corner of Seventh Avenue and St. John's Place. Though free-spirited in his youth, the entrepreneurially inclined Engeman (b. 1840) became rich selling horses and mules to the Union army during the Civil War.[113] He moved to Brooklyn soon thereafter, eventually taking up residence at number 44 Seventh Avenue (built 1881). In 1878, he purchased several hundred acres of Brooklyn oceanfront, which he named Brighton Beach, and provided several lucrative improvements, including a pier, hotel and bath. He opened the racetrack in 1879, and it was earning him some $2 million a year by 1882. He died of Bright's (i.e. kidney) disease at home on August 12, 1884, and left his estate to his son William and brother George. William continued his father's business interests and later moved to 119 St. John's Place, while George moved to number 123 St. John's. The elder Engeman's daughter later married one of Gaynor's law partners.

By the late 1890s, Sportsmen's Row was, for all intents and purposes, a designation in name alone. Mike Dwyer, Snapper Garrison and James Rowe had all moved on, and Phil Dwyer was seldom to be seen in number 8. Though Pinkerton, Hyde and Shevlin would remain on Eighth Avenue, horse racing was largely peripheral to their identities. Instead, the block was now dominated by the likes of William Gaynor, Mirabeau Towns and the

Fureys. At the same time, the concept of Sportsmen's Row would not only persist but also take on even greater significance. It would soon constitute a rallying cry around which its residents would unite to preserve the very integrity of their block.

SPITE ROW AND THE NEW CENTURY, 1901–1914

In early 1897, Edward Dodge and his family moved to 12 Eighth Avenue.[114] Dodge had purchased the house from James Rowe, who, returning to training, had been largely absent from Sportsmen's Row in the last few years of his residence. Dodge was a successful banker, and number 12 was a perfect residence in which to display his status. He and his wife, Ida, would blend seamlessly into life on Eighth Avenue; he was a prominent member of the Montauk and several other exclusive clubs, while her Wednesday morning euchre games, played in the parlor, were popular among the neighborhood wives. The Dodge family was taking its place among Brooklyn's elite, and the view from their new home—across Grand Army Plaza to the park beyond—was one of the most desirable.

Unbeknownst to Dodge, he was about to lose that vista. The thin parcel of land that had made the unobstructed view possible—on the east side of the block between the Montauk Club and Hyde and Behman's apartment building—had been the focus of an ongoing tussle between the residents of Sportsmen's Row and one of Park Slope's most prolific builders, Charles Peterson. Mayor Chapin had once owned the 75- by 100-foot parcel and had incorporated a number of building restrictions in its deed.[115] He later sold the plot, and after changing hands several times, it came into Peterson's possession by 1895. In June of that year, Peterson obtained a permit to build a row of houses with frontages along both Eighth Avenue

Sportsmen's Row, 1929. *Photo by Percy Loomis Sperr ©Milstein Division, the New York Public Library.*

and Plaza Streets. Although their views would have been obstructed, the residents of Sportsmen's Row offered no opposition to the plan. Peterson, however, undertook no construction, and the permit expired.

SPITE ROW

In June 1896, Peterson submitted new plans for the lot, but this time with houses facing only Plaza Street.[116] It was an alarming turn of events. As the *Brooklyn Daily Eagle* reported, "The residents of Sportsmen's Row on Eighth Avenue, between St. Johns and Lincoln places, are very much disturbed over the prospect that C.G. Peterson places before them." Not only would they lose their view, but they would also have it replaced by unsightly rear lots and fences.

Sportsmen's Row banded together and, under the advisement of Mirabeau Towns, appealed to the commissioner of buildings to reject the permits. As Peterson's applications were in order, the request was denied. Next, William Gubbins—resident of number 16, builder of numbers 12–18 and something of Peterson's competitor—filed a restraining order on June 27 to prevent his rival from breaking ground. Gubbins claimed that the terms of Chapin's original deed indicated that any houses built on the land had to face Eighth Avenue. On July 8, the injunction was enforced. Though the presiding judge could not identify a specific declaration in the deed, he ruled that its intent (which did specify high-class housing) suggested as much. On Sportsmen's Row, the ruling was met with relief, particularly as its residents had come to believe that Peterson had no intention of actually building his houses but was rather goading them to buy the parcel at unfavorable terms. On December 12, the injunction was made permanent, and round one went to Sportsmen's Row.

Peterson, however, was undeterred, and the case slowly made its way up through the courts. The injunction was later vacated—the case was, after all, rather flimsy—and the residents of Sportsmen's Row, with Gaynor now joining Towns in counsel, appealed. They were subsequently defeated in the appellate court and then, finally, in the court of appeals. Peterson's hand was freed.[117]

In the late summer of 1900, Peterson dispatched a team of laborers to the site. They worked slowly, in what may have been a last-ditch attempt to prompt a favorable buyout by the residents of Sportsmen's Row. No such offer was forthcoming, and in early 1901, Peterson dispatched a phalanx of workers to begin work in earnest. The construction became the talk of the neighborhood, and "at almost any hour of the day a group of men...could be seen on the Eighth Avenue walking before the plot, talking, gesticulating and pointing with their walking sticks at the different parts of the rapidly deepening cellars."[118] The block's residents tried pleading, reasoning and even threatening Peterson, who never lost his composure and countered that his actions were entirely legal and in full compliance with the property's deed. Sportsmen's Row was, as the *Brooklyn Daily Eagle* put it, "violated and invaded and helpless to resist the invader."[119]

With time running out, Gaynor called an emergency meeting at the Montauk Club. Peterson was formally (and finally) approached about selling and, after some waffling, set a price of $32,000. It was steep, considering the land had been assessed at no more than $20,000. The group then determined that, if they could not buy the land outright, Peterson might be persuaded to reorient the houses for the consideration of $12,000. Gaynor immediately offered up $1,000, as did seven other residents of Sportsmen's Row. It was hoped that the balance would be provided by the Montauk Club, which—as Gaynor noted—would also be negatively impacted by Peterson's new houses.

At the club, however, the members were split over whether to provide the $4,000 balance. Many of the members did not live nearby and felt it an unfair imposition. The club's directors were in something of a bind and, trying to please both sides, offered only $1,000 to the collection. Sportsmen's Row was outraged. Its residents withdrew their contributions and threatened secession from the Montauk Club. As one anonymous resident explained to the *Eagle*, "Why we should we pay our money for the benefit of our stingy, if not mean, big neighbor, the Montauk Club?" He also stated that with Peterson's plans moving forward, he had every intention of selling his house on Sportsmen's Row. As for Peterson, he held firm to his final offer; as his nephew affirmed, the houses were to be finished "as soon as the weather would permit, unless the people up there decide to pay his price."[120]

There was to be no last-minute reprieve for Sportsmen's Row. That fall, Peterson's houses were completed in full compliance with Mayor Chapin's original restrictions: elegant in character and four-stories in height but facing onto the park circle and with rear yards abutting Eighth Avenue. From Plaza Street, the four, designed by Frederick Tyrrell in the Neoclassical style, compose a stunning set of tall, narrow limestone town houses.[121] Along Eighth Avenue, however, their rear elevations and backyards present a jarring sight. Following their completion, the houses were christened Spite Row "because they turn their backs on Sportsmen's Row."[122]

The anonymous resident of Sportsmen's Row quoted by the *Eagle* was, in fact, Edward Dodge. Dodge made good on his threat and unloaded number 12 in October 1901 for $17,000—an amount notably lower than Rowe's original purchase price ($18,000 in 1891) and $1,000 less than the mortgage Dodge himself had taken out on the property in 1897. He had been on Eighth Avenue for only a short time, but the *Eagle* noted his departure to Queens as the "first break for a number of years in the ownership of 'Sportsmen's Row,' and...coincidental with the first sale of what has become known as 'Spite Row' on the opposite side of Eighth Avenue."

Spite Row and the New Century, 1901–1914

The sale also provided the *Brooklyn Daily Eagle* an opportunity to relate the history of the block, as well as a snapshot of all of the block's residents in the fall of 1901:[123]

> *The present owners of this row, beginning at no. 8, at the corner of St. Johns Place and running to no. 26, at Lincoln Place, are as follows: Joseph A. McGarry* [number 8], *son of famous alderman of earlier days, and a brother of Councilman John J. McGarry. Joseph A. McGarry married the daughter of Philip Dwyer, who then owned the corner, but who a few years ago presented it to his daughter. Robert Furey* [number 10], *the well-known contractor and politician; "Val" Schmitt,* [number 12's] *new owner, now well known in sporting circles; Mrs. George G. Browne* [number 14]*, William Gubbins* [number 16]*, an extensive builder in Brooklyn; Carl Goepel* [number 18]*; Supreme Court Judge William*

"Spite Row," facing onto the park circle, 1914. To the right is the apartment building once owned by Hyde & Behman. *Courtesy of New York Transit Museum.*

"Spite Row" from Eighth Avenue, 1905. The Montauk Club is on the right, and the Hyde & Behman apartment building is on the far left. *Courtesy of the Milstein Division of United States History, Local History & Genealogy, New York Public Library.*

> *J. Gaynor* [number 20], *Richard Hyde* [number 22], *the head of the theatrical firm of Hyde and Behman, and a controlling factor in the vaudeville trust; Lawyer Mirabeau Towns* [number 24], *and ex-Judge James Troy* [number 26], *whose house, the south corner, was owned originally by Michael Dwyer…*

By the turn of the century, Sportsmen's Row was largely absent of sportsmen, but it was still home to sundry characters who brought continued charisma to this remarkable stretch of Eighth Avenue. A number of them had lived on the block since its inception, and a handful had been, at one time or another, associates and friends of the sportsmen.

JOSEPH McGARRY, NUMBER 8 EIGHTH AVENUE

Joseph McGarry's 1893 marriage to Phil Dwyer's daughter Lydia had proved a happy one. Though Phil had little to do with local Prospect Heights society, his daughter attended the prestigious Packer Institute and later became active in a number of charities and organizations, including the Brooklyn Institute of the Arts and Sciences (the predecessor of the Brooklyn Museum). Her husband, meanwhile, had followed in the footsteps of his father-in-law and established his own racing operation in the summer of 1900.[124] Partnering with his brother John, the McGarry stable raced under the colors of light blue with black dots. Given McGarry's family pedigree, expectations were high as to the stable's outlook.

The McGarry-Dwyer marriage, however, would ultimately prove tragic and short-lived. The couple had lost two children in infancy, and Lydia—like her brother before her—was stricken with tuberculosis in early 1901. That summer, the family made their way to Saratoga in the hopes that the country air might spur a recovery. Instead, she took a turn for the worse and died on October 27 with her father, husband and infant daughter at her side.[125] The family returned to Brooklyn, where their beloved Lydia was memorialized at St. Augustine and laid to rest in the family plot at the Cemetery of the Holy Cross.

Phil Dwyer and Joseph McGarry departed number 8 almost immediately thereafter, though the house wasn't put on the market until November 1902. McGarry and his infant daughter moved in with his brother (and former racing partner) John, who, having just become president of the Cuban-American Tobacco Company, was seemingly on the fast track to success.

Joseph McGarry's new living arrangement, however, also proved short-lived, as his brother died of complications of pneumonia on February 22, 1902, at their home on 176 Nevins Street.[126] Grief aside, the surviving family members had expected a handsome payout from his estate. John, however, was not just dead, but dead broke. Upon investigation, it was discovered that his estate, which had appeared so robust, was actually some $200,000 in debt and plagued by serious questions about the legality of its outstanding loans and mortgages. Friends were at a loss to explain the discrepancy, though some keen observers noted that the first (and, as it turned out, only) year of the brothers' racing operation had been a competitive and financial failure.

McGarry would eventually regain his footing and remarry. He would also remain in contact with his former father-in-law and racing mentor and was in attendance at his funeral in 1917.

THE FUREYS, NUMBER 10 EIGHTH AVENUE

The Furey brothers, William and Robert, had been a staple on Sportsmen's Row since the completion of numbers 8–10 in December 1892. From the start, they had functioned as something of a bridge between the block's sportsmen and politicians. Robert, a builder, was a close friend of the Dwyers, while William was a celebrated fixture in local Democratic politics. Both brothers had wrestled with health issues—their 1898 bout with a serious attack of the grip (influenza) warranted mention twice by the *Brooklyn Daily Eagle*[127]—but they had remained outgoing, committed and esteemed in their respective fields. On June 28, 1900, their fraternal bond was shattered when the sixty-eight-year-old William died of "paralysis"—a condition from which he had apparently suffered numerous attacks over the past several years.[128] His widow, Matilda, remained at number 10 but followed her husband to the grave a little less than two years later (on June 4, 1902).[129] As with the Dwyer family, St. Augustine played host to their funerals.

Following William and Matilda's deaths, Robert invited his younger brother John and John's wife to come and live with him at number 10. John had been residing in Philadelphia and, though a native of Brooklyn, had spent most of his life in the military. He had enlisted in the Eighty-fourth New York Infantry at the outbreak of the Civil War and had become a captain and assistant quartermaster soon after its conclusion. He subsequently served out West, seeing much action in the Indian Wars. At the time of his retirement, he had achieved the rank of brigadier general.

The living arrangement eventually proved less than ideal, and in 1909 Robert departed number 10 and took up residence in the Montauk Club. Neither brother betrayed an exact cause for the separation, but several acquaintances referenced an argument over Robert having fed expensive lamb chops to his dog. Others suggested that Robert, a staunch Catholic, was never able to accept the presence of John's Protestant wife. Regardless, the split was seemingly irreparable, and Robert's peculiarities permitted fanciful speculation as to its cause.

Robert was a perpetual bachelor, and the only woman with whom he had ever been close was his mother. He neither drank nor smoked, and though he had many acquaintances, he was something of a mystery to them. His religiosity was well known, but there were also vague rumors about other types of company that he kept. By the time of his move to the Montauk Club, he was well into his seventies, and he spent much of his time there playing cards. He continued to find games of chance appealing, just as he had enjoyed betting on horses in the previous decade when he was so often found in the company of the Dwyers.

Robert had also become quite wealthy, having parlayed his work as a contractor into being the chief stockholder of the Cranford Company, a large cement manufacturer. He also held a large number of shares in the Gravesend and Aqueduct racetracks. Eccentricities aside (or perhaps because of them), he was remarkably generous with his riches. Despite their apparent disagreement, he gave his brother number 10 and also purchased homes for two of his nieces.[130] On Christmas Day 1912, he donated $100,000 to the Catholic charities administered by the bishop of Long Island (who also received, at the same time, an identical amount from James Shevlin for the support of Brooklyn's St. Mary's Hospital).[131]

On March 12, 1913, Robert Furey died at the age of eighty in his fourth-floor suite at the Montauk Club.[132] The terminal illness of his final days had engendered a small rapprochement between the brothers, and his body was carried across the street and laid out at number 10. In the grand parlor, his life was recalled and honored by a wide circle of acquaintances, former colleagues and family members. Several days later, the contents of his will were disclosed. Though he was survived by his brother and ten nieces and nephews, Robert left the entirety of his estate—estimated to be worth between $1 and $2 million—to an old political associate, John Morrissey Gray, the Democratic leader of the Eighth Assembly District and so-called Duke of Gowanus. Though Furey and Gray had been close, it was entirely unexpected. Needless to say, John Furey contested the will, though eventually settled in October 1913 for the consideration of $65,000. Robert's previous generosity (specifically his transfer of number 10) seems to have been a mitigating factor in reaching a settlement. For his part, John Furey remained in number 10 until his death at age seventy-six on December 17, 1914.[133] The house was put on the market a short time later.

VALENTINE SCHMITT, NUMBER 12 EIGHTH AVENUE

By 1901, number 12 was home to its third owner in less than ten years. Trainer Rowe had sold the house in 1897 to Edward Dodge, who in turn sold it to Valentine Schmitt soon after the completion of Spite Row.[134] Schmitt was something of a departure from the refined Dodge, which may have colored the *Eagle*'s aforementioned description of his purchase as a "break" in ownership. Schmitt was a first-generation immigrant, entrepreneur and self-made made man—none of which was necessarily uncommon on Eighth Avenue—but he had done so as the reigning king of Brooklyn's freewheeling late-night tavern and saloon scene. That, on the other hand, was far less typical.

Valentin Schmitt was born in Germany in 1857 and immigrated to the United Stated in 1876. Soon after his arrival, he adopted the anglicized form of his name (Valentine) but was generally called "Val." He married his first wife, Katharine Huff, in 1884. They took up residence in Brooklyn Heights and became members of the nearby Zion Lutheran Church, which was a focal point for many German immigrants (and which has maintained its tradition as a German-speaking congregation to this day). Soon thereafter, Schmitt became a successful restaurateur, opening a series of profitable operations throughout Brooklyn and, later, beyond. When he moved to Sportsmen's Row in 1901 with his wife, four children and two servants, he was also on the verge of becoming the president of the Federal Brewing Company, one of the many contemporary breweries that called Brooklyn home. Though the company would go belly up and be bought out in 1907, its grand production plant at the corner of Third Avenue and Dean Street still stands. In the long-standing tradition of Sportsmen's Row, state Supreme Court justice Gaynor had some involvement with the company's final dispensation, affirming a decision on the timing of a hearing on the value of its stock.[135] In 1905, Schmitt would open his most famous establishment, the Hof Bräu Haus, at 588 Fulton Street—right across the street from Percy Williams's grand Orpheum Theater.[136]

Schmitt was a rotund, gregarious fellow who thrived on the wanton atmosphere of his establishments. He was often accompanied by an entourage and advertised his Hof Bräu Haus as the "coolest place in the city" with "tables reserved for ladies." He was also known for his lavish theme parties and several namesake dishes (such as Veal à la Schmitt). Success permitted him introduction to many of the city's movers and shakers, including John

Valentine Schmitt's Hof Bräu Haus.

Hylan, a longtime Bushwick resident and eventual mayor of New York City (1918–25), who would later appoint Schmitt an honorary deputy commissioner of the Parks Department. An avid horseman, Schmitt used the post to advocate for the improvement of Prospect Park's bridle paths.

Schmitt would spend almost thirty years at number 12 and leave a lasting mark of his long residency. Soon after moving in, he remodeled the dining room, paneling it with a severe wooden wainscoting. Though Arts and Craft in style, the feeling is that of a Bavarian lodge. The house would also play host to a number of elaborate affairs, including a dual party in October 1905 that celebrated both Schmitt's daughter Elfrieda's twentieth birthday party and the grand opening of his latest Manhattan *rathskeller*.[137] It would also witness two tragedies: his wife, Katharine, died there on April 15, 1915, as did his only son, the twenty-two-year-old Valentine Otto Frederick, of pneumonia on the morning of Tuesday, March 6, 1917.[138]

Two of Schmitt's daughters would continue to reside with him at number 12. In April 1928, their filial piety would be tested when Valentine—at the ripe old age of seventy-two—remarried one Dorothea Graff, whom he had known for less than a year and, even more scandalously, was some thirty-seven years his junior (though on the marriage certificate Schmitt did claim to be a sprightly fifty-eight years old). His daughters were distraught, one comparing it to an infamous contemporary scandal (the marriage of sixteen-year-old actress Frances Belle Heenan [aka "Peaches"] to Edward Browning, a fifty-one-year-old real estate magnate):[139] "He did this in a sneaky way and we are very upset over it. It's just another case of Peaches and Browning. How could such a young woman really be in love with father?" Their father's second wedding ceremony was a low-key affair held at the home of the bride's mother, with only one old friend of Schmitt's attending on his behalf. The newlyweds honeymooned in Atlantic City and later sailed to Europe. Life in number 12 was irrevocably fractured, and the house was subdivided and rented out in August 1930.[140]

Schmitt's second marriage was destined to fail, and he would eventually reconcile with his family.[141] On July 23, 1939, his children and grandchildren celebrated his eighty-third birthday at the landmark Old '76 House in Tappan, New York. The family patriarch passed away on March 24, 1944, joining his first wife and son in the family plot in Brooklyn's famous Green-Wood Cemetery.

GEORGE BROWNE, NUMBER 14 EIGHTH AVENUE

Mrs. George G. Browne (née Clotilde Gimbrède) was a relative newcomer to Sportsmen's Row. She had moved there in 1899 following her marriage to George Browne, a partner in the dry goods firm of Amory, Browne & Co. Browne had lived at number 14 since 1893, and though rich (his income was believed to be on the order of $50,000 per year), he was something of an introvert. His only marriage was later in life, and to a widow (Clotilde) with an older son. He was also given to anxiety and hypochondria.

In April 1900, the fifty-six-year-old Browne began to feel ill; he had various vague symptoms, but after his vision faltered he sought out an oculist for treatment.[142] The doctor diagnosed him with Bright's disease, which unnerved the high-strung Browne. He became obsessed with the diagnosis, reading all the medical information that he could obtain and worrying endlessly to his friends and colleagues. At their suggestion, he sought out second, third and fourth opinions, all of which contradicted the initial diagnosis. Rather than offering reassurance, Browne grew more despondent with each passing day.

In the early morning hours of Wednesday, June 6, Browne's wife lay asleep in the back bedroom on the second floor of number 14. Her sleep was fractured, frequently interrupted by her husband shuffling about in the adjoining front bedroom. Sometime between three and four o'clock in the morning, she was aroused by a gunshot. She hurried down the hallway to her husband's bedroom, where she found him bleeding profusely from the head, a smoking revolver at his side. Her son, also coming upon the scene, ran outside and down St. John's Place to 14 Seventh Avenue, the residence of their family doctor. The doctor returned with him to Eighth Avenue and pronounced Browne dead at the scene. Clotilde remained in number 14 until her death in 1914, whereupon the house became the possession of her son, Louis Gimbrède, who departed in 1919.

William H. Gubbins, Number 16 Eighth Avenue

William Gubbins's spirited defense of Sportsmen's Row during the Peterson saga was to prove the final act in what had been a successful career as a builder. On Tuesday, August 30, 1904, he died of pneumonia at the age of sixty-nine.[143] He passed away at home, where he was memorialized in a small service that Saturday and buried in Green-Wood Cemetery.

Gubbins was a first-generation immigrant, born into an affluent family in Dublin on February 13, 1835.[144] When a young man, he immigrated to the United States, immediately establishing himself in Brooklyn as a builder and contractor. At the outbreak of the Civil War, he joined the Union army, which appointed him a chief clerk and manager on Governor's Island. Following the war, he returned to the building trade and married Louis Moore (1867), whose family proudly traced its ancestry back to the Revolutionary War. He soon earned a reputation as a highly competent builder, particularly in the area of Prospect Heights. The speed and efficiency of his operations—he would obtain land, quickly erect high-quality housing and promptly sell the upgraded properties—brought him great financial and popular success. As with many of his neighbors, he was a fixture in local society, belonging to several local clubs and organizations.

Gubbins had lived on Sportsmen's Row almost from its inception. He had built four of its houses (numbers 12–18) and had also tried to sell number 27 to President Cleveland in 1889. His 1891 move to number 16 was quite sensible, as the block was already considered one of the most exclusive in Brooklyn.

CARL GOEPEL, NUMBER 18 EIGHTH AVENUE

Valentine Schmitt was not the first native-born German to reside on the block. Since its completion in 1891, number 18 had been home to Carl Goepel, who was born in Stuttgart in 1847.[145] Unlike Schmitt, Goepel's profession was considerably more refined. After immigrating to the United States and settling in Brooklyn in 1864, he became a banker. In 1873, he joined the distinguished New York banking firm of Shultz & Ruckgaber and, after demonstrating his managerial and financial acumen, worked his way up to become director of the Germania Savings Bank and the Germania Life Insurance Company.

Though Goepel was counted in the city's leading social circles, he was most active within the German-American patriciate. He was an energetic member of the exclusive Germania Club, which, founded in 1859, was one of Brooklyn's oldest social organizations. He was the club's vice-president in 1884 and 1885 and its president in 1888, 1889 and 1893. Under his leadership, the club moved from its rather pedestrian headquarters at 127 Atlantic Avenue to a new clubhouse at 120 Schermerhorn Street (between Smith Street and Boerum Place). Designed by acclaimed Brooklyn architect Frank Freeman (1861–October 13, 1949), the new edifice was, in the words of a contemporary pundit, "as a specimen of Romanesque architecture...unsurpassed by any other structure in Brooklyn."[146] It was an imposing four-story building fashioned of brownstone, light-colored brick and terra cotta. Its façade was lavishly carved, while its interior was finely appointed and outfitted with a range of amenities. It was, in short, an architectural masterpiece, but one ultimately short-lived. The building was demolished in the 1920s to clear space for the IND (now A and C) subway line.

Goepel and his wife, Mathilde, had two children, a son and a daughter (a third son died in infancy). Their daughter, Elsa Clara (b. 1879), was the object of much fancy by the young men of the neighborhood, and the Goepels hosted several parties in her honor in number 18, including a well-

The Germania Club. *Courtesy of the Milstein Division of United States History, Local History & Genealogy, New York Public Library.*

attended dance in January 1899. Tragically, her beauty proved fleeting and her life all too brief. She died of pemphigus, a horribly disfiguring autoimmune disease, on January 9, 1901, at the age of twenty-one.[147] She was memorialized in a small service at number 18 and laid to rest in Green-Wood Cemetery on Saturday, January 12. After a year in virtual seclusion, the Goepels returned to their active social lives and remained in number 18 for another decade. They then moved to the Hotel Bossert in Brooklyn Heights and later to Manhattan's Riverside Drive. Carl passed away on July 24, 1931, and Mathilde on April 21, 1932. In death, they were reunited with their beloved Elsa in Green-Wood.

RICHARD HYDE, NUMBER 22 EIGHTH AVENUE

Richard Hyde had found continued success in vaudeville. In 1899, he and Behman consolidated their holdings under the auspices of the Hyde and Behman Amusement Company, the name under which Hyde continued operating after Behman's death in 1902. By 1906, Hyde was running a number of national theaters, including four in Brooklyn alone. He also maintained his significant investment in the Brooklyn Jockey Club and, like Robert Furey, represented something of a last link to the block's heyday of sportsmen.

Hyde and his wife, Mary, had four children in number 22: three girls and a boy. The family was popular and well known throughout Brooklyn, and the house played frequent host to all manner of parties and engagements. They were a close-knit group and, beyond Richard's association with the Brooklyn Jockey Club, shared an interest in sport and physical recreation. Golf, in particular, was their game, and though Richard was known for his prowess on the links, he was no match for his daughter Lillian. Born in 1888, Lillian had early on distinguished herself in all types of athleticism, particularly those involving a racket or on horseback. She was a particularly outstanding golf player and would later win five Women's Amateur Metropolitan Golf championships.[148] After Snapper Garrison and James McLaughlin, she was the most successful athlete to make her residence on Sportsmen's Row.

Richard Hyde lived out his final years on Eighth Avenue. Falling ill in late 1912, he went to Tucson in the hopes that the weather might ameliorate his deteriorating health. Instead, he died there on December 14, 1912.[149] He left an estate valued at $1,245,487, which included his residence on Eighth Avenue, another on Bay Shore, three Brooklyn theaters and 575 shares in the Brooklyn Jockey Club. His holdings were split among his wife and four children, with an additional $25,000 bequeathed to the Actor's Fund of America.[150] Mary Hyde departed soon thereafter, first to her summer home in Bay Shore and later to Manhattan, where she died on December 27, 1917.[151]

Hyde's death, however, would soon become nothing more than a footnote in the history of the block. In the following year, its most famous resident would pass away, and in something of a final act on a national stage, Sportsmen's Row would play a most prominent role in his memorialization.

THE MAYOR

William James Gaynor was born near Oriskany, New York, probably in the month of February and likely in the year 1847.[152] He was subsequently rather elusive about many details of his personal life, which permitted him to "play up" some of the particulars or downplay others. His father, for instance, was an Irish immigrant named Keiron, whose name Gaynor later Anglicized to the more patrician "Kendrick." Though Keiron was a blacksmith, Gaynor and his five siblings lived on a farm that provided much of their basic needs. While Gaynor found solace and comfort in the rustic life, he was generally ill suited for the hard work and manual labor that it entailed. Rather, he early on demonstrated an interest in and aptitude toward more cerebral pursuits.

The Gaynors were observant Catholics, and every Sunday the family piled into their wagon and attended Mass in neighboring Utica. As a boy, Gaynor was particularly devout and took much pleasure in the New Testament and Christian teachings. Accordingly, his parents enrolled him in the Assumption Academy in Utica, a Christian Brothers institution. Under the brothers' encouragement, Gaynor subsequently entered the novitiate of the brotherhood at the De la Salle Institute in New York City on December 17, 1863.

Gaynor spent the next five years in the Christian Brothers, including teaching stints in St. Louis and Baltimore. In the summer of 1868, he and six other brothers set out to staff the newly established St. Mary's College in San Francisco. At some point on the trip, Gaynor had a crisis of confidence—not

William Gaynor on the stoop of number 20 Eighth Avenue.

so much in his faith (that would come later) but more for his suitability to a religious life. He consequently left the order and returned to Utica. He had taken no vows, and his departure was apparently without incident.

Upon returning home, Gaynor took up study of the law. Given his intellect and education, he soon found a position in the law offices of Horatio and John Seymour, Utica's most prestigious firm. Horatio Seymour was also the city's most illustrious son. Former mayor and Democratic governor of the state, he had just narrowly lost the presidential election to the Republican Ulysses S. Grant (by 300,000 votes). In the following year, Gaynor moved to the office of Judge Ward Hunt, also a former mayor of the city and an eventual Supreme Court justice. These were formative years in Gaynor's professional development. To his academic and literary interests (of which he considered the Bible, *Don Quixote* and Benjamin Franklin's *Autobiography* his favorites) were now added politics and public service (and a predilection for the Democratic Party). Under Hunt's tutelage, Gaynor was admitted to the New York Bar in 1871.

Setting out on his own, Gaynor moved to Boston in the fall of 1872. He found little professional success there, and what meager work he could find apparently involved chasing down delinquent accounts. He did however like the city's orderly manner, lifestyle and sense of community, and that weighed heavily in his thoughts about a subsequent destination. So, eschewing the conventional wisdom that success as a lawyer could best be found in New York City, he chose instead the city to its immediate east: Brooklyn, whither he moved in 1873.

Unfortunately, Gaynor arrived at a difficult time. The country was entering a prolonged depression, and under- and unemployed lawyers abounded. Accordingly, Judge Hunt provided Gaynor a letter of introduction to St. Clair McKelway, the editor of the *Brooklyn Daily Eagle*. McKelway was suitably impressed by Gaynor but had little to offer at the *Eagle*. He was, however, able to help him obtain a position at the rival *Brooklyn Argus*. Gaynor received a salary of fifteen dollars per week and moved to a boardinghouse at 38 First Place. He soon proved himself a solid, if dispassionate, writer whose legal skills and temperament served him well in the role.

At the *Argus*, Gaynor largely conducted himself in a most formal manner, with one remarkable exception. In July 1874, and seemingly out of nowhere, he applied for a warrant to arrest Theodore Tilton, who had accused the famous abolitionist Henry Ward Beecher of having an affair with his wife. Gaynor's charge was that Tilton's accusation amounted to slander. The legal maneuver was highly unorthodox, and the judge repeatedly pressed

Gaynor to drop the charge. After several adjournments, the court requested that Gaynor receive a writ of mandamus from the state Supreme Court in order to proceed. Gaynor failed to do so, and the case was eventually dropped (in the following year, Tilton would sue Beecher in court, though the jury would be unable to reach a verdict; Julian Ralph, who would later mention northern Eighth Avenue in *Harper's*, covered the trial extensively). Why Gaynor leveled the charge is a mystery, and the only explanation that he ever offered was that he felt obligated to pursue justice. There was some speculation that he was pushed by the editor of the *Argus* (who supported Tilton and may have wanted to move the case to the courts) or that he was seeking publicity for his legal skills. The peculiarity of the incident may also indicate nothing more than something of an idealistic naïveté. Soon after the incident, the *Argus* folded, and Gaynor began writing for the *New York Sun* and Flatbush's the *Independent*.

In the fall of 1874, Gaynor married Emma Vesta Hyde and moved to the town of Flatbush (then independent from the city of Brooklyn). On the occasion, he officially changed his middle name from James to Jay and his father's from Keiron to Kendrick. It was here that Gaynor gained some traction as a lawyer, and he soon developed a diverse portfolio of clients and legal competencies. He represented everyone from the town drunk to the local temperance society and soon established his credentials as a knowledgeable, methodical and formidable lawyer. Regarding his evolving persona, one of Gaynor's principle biographers noted that he was[153]

> a lone wolf who worked best alone, quiet, usually taciturn, meticulous in preparation and presentation of a case; in court he was rather fond of literary allusions and a sometimes heavy-handed sarcasm, but behind the rather underplayed theatrics always well informed and certain of his law.

He was becoming almost the opposite of his more charismatic friend (and future neighbor in number 24), the "poet-lawyer" Mirabeau Towns, who was also establishing his own legal career at the time.

It was in Flatbush that Gaynor also got his first real taste of Brooklyn's rancorous and corrupt machine politics. Success had brought him clients outside the village, including the neighboring towns of Gravesend and New Lots. Gravesend was an old foundation, established in 1643 by Lady Deborah Moody and originally intended as an Anabaptist refuge. It would have remained relatively inconsequential save that it happened to include an oceanfront district known as Coney Island. As a result, Gravesend generated wealth and power far in excess of its size. It was also ruled by the infamous John Y. McKane, one of the most powerful and ruthless of political bosses. Simultaneously both doting family man and pitiless enforcer, McKane worked tirelessly to ensure that the money streaming into his coffers from Coney Island kept the residents of Gravesend his loyal and willing subjects. He officially held a number of positions, including town supervisor and chief of police, but it was his oversight of the Land Board of Gravesend that permitted him much deft scheming and manipulation. Gaynor was hired as the board's counsel, and it was in this role that he faced (and defeated) his future neighbor, builder Robert Furey, in the courts. McKane's chicanery was well known, but Gaynor betrayed no apparent reluctance with the association. Later, however, as Gaynor's identity as a reformer took hold, the two would find themselves bitter enemies.

Of greater embarrassment to Gaynor was his 1881 divorce on the grounds of adultery. The reason was particularly scandalous given Gaynor's Catholicism, though it was at the time the only reason granted a divorce by the state. The union had at least been childless, so Gaynor was spared the necessity of providing child support, and the break could be a clean one. Nonetheless, it would continue to dog him for decades and foster much personal resentment toward a condemnatory church. Gaynor ultimately remained rather mum on the details but accepted full blame and responsibility for the disunion. Given his manner and work ethic, "irreconcilable differences" probably best describes its cause.

By 1886, Gaynor had settled down sufficiently enough to remarry, taking as his wife Augusta C. Meyer, the daughter of a wealthy carriage maker from Belleville, New Jersey. The couple moved back to Brooklyn and took up residence in 212 St. John's Place, just around the corner from Sportsmen's Row, which—though it hadn't yet officially earned the moniker—was already home to Mike Dwyer and Jockey McLaughlin. Gaynor opened a practice on Montague Street with two other successful attorneys, and their firm soon became one of the busiest and most successful in the city. Gaynor personally attracted a number of important clients, including Abraham Abraham, whom he advised on the establishment (with Nathan and Isidor Straus) of the seminal retail outfit Abraham & Straus in 1893 (Isidor and his wife would later die aboard the *Titanic*). Another of his clients was Sarah F. McMahon, Snapper Garrison's mother-in-law, who had sued the jockey in January 1890 to dissolve their racing partnership (a case that Gaynor saw decided favorably on her behalf).

Of all Gaynor's A-list clients, however, none was more important than William Ziegler, the baking powder king. Ziegler (September 1, 1843–May 25, 1905) had made a fortune as one of the principals of the Royal Baking Powder Company. After a later falling out with his partners, he retained Gaynor to handle the legal separation, which proved a daunting and complex affair. Gaynor and Ziegler were ultimately triumphant, and Ziegler, after selling off his interests in the corporation, purchased several smaller companies. He subsequently built up a conglomerate large enough to eventually buy out the Royal Baking Powder Company and establish a baking powder "trust," which yielded him tens of millions of dollars. In addition to more idiosyncratic interests in arctic exploration and yachting, Ziegler also had a zeal for political reform (as a businessman, he was admittedly somewhat less principled). And so, on Ziegler's behalf, Gaynor undertook a series of cases that would ultimately solidify his credentials as a top legal mind and establish his reputation as an aggressive and effective political reformer.

In 1889–90, Ziegler and Gaynor went after a questionable agreement that the city had made to buy the Long Island Water Company in advance of its annexation of the town of New Lots. The company was valued at no more than $195,000, but city officials had agreed to purchase it for $1,250,000. Gaynor and Ziegler investigated the deal and exposed a whole slew of questionable dealings and characters. Mayor Chapin came out looking particularly bad, and his obfuscation of the matter only increased Gaynor and Ziegler's desire to pursue justice. At the time, Chapin was at the height of his popularity and living on Sportsmen's Row. Ziegler and Gaynor's efforts, however, would usher something of a reversal. Chapin's political star would begin to fall, while Gaynor's would start to rise—so much so that soon thereafter Gaynor would be briefly floated as a possible Republican challenger to Chapin in the upcoming mayoral election. Though Ziegler and Gaynor ultimately won the case on a technicality, they came away widely perceived as champions of the city's taxpayers.

Two additional cases in 1892 further buttressed Gaynor's reformist credentials. One involved the payment of back taxes by the elevated railroad companies (which argued that they had been over-assessed and chose not to pay; an agreement was eventually reached), while the other blocked the city comptroller from paying the exorbitant bills submitted by city officials in celebration of the 400th anniversary of Columbus's voyage to America. The subject of the latter lawsuit even made it as far as the state legislature, which passed a bill to fund the politicians' profligacy. Gaynor interceded directly with Governor Roswell P. Flower, who subsequently vetoed the bill. It was a tremendous victory for Gaynor and Ziegler. In many ways, Ziegler was ultimately responsible for "making" Gaynor a political force and for "directing" his political energies toward the work of reform.

In 1893, popular sentiment in Brooklyn was profoundly antiestablishment, in part because of the duplicity that Gaynor and Ziegler had exposed. Gaynor's efforts had made him profoundly popular among the citizenry but almost as equally distasteful to the party machines. The Democrats, in particular, resented the damage done to Chapin and his successor, David Boody (mayor, 1892–93; he lived nearby at 204 Berkeley Place). The Republicans found him slightly less objectionable and, though he leaned Democratic, nominated him on their ticket for the New York State Supreme Court; his popularity and intellect also figured to provide an effective counterbalance to their otherwise uninspiring mayoral candidate, Charles Schieren. Gaynor had actually desired the mayoralty, but his hostility to party politics made this all but impossible. In a speech that Gaynor contemporaneously delivered at Manhattan's Delmonico's Restaurant to the board of trade, he had suggested that "in New York men are concerned in politics, in Brooklyn, only fools."[154]

After much deliberation, Gaynor accepted the Republican nomination for Supreme Court justice. Popularity aside, one major impediment potentially stood in his way: Gaynor's old associate, John McKane. McKane had so effectively padded the Gravesend electoral rolls that the small town had the potential to sway elections, even national ones. In the 1888 presidential race, Grover Cleveland had lost New York State by only one thousand votes; at the time, McKane had been angry with the Democratic Party and delivered all of Gravesend's six thousand votes to Benjamin Harrison, the eventual victor. In 1893, McKane stood unreservedly for the Democratic ticket. Though he seems to have had no personal issues with Gaynor—the two of them after all had been colleagues for a good number of years—it was Gaynor's newfound reformist mantle to which he objected.

Gaynor bided his time. Two weeks before the election, he requested a writ of mandamus to force the Gravesend authorities to permit an inspection of their electoral lists. The mandamus was rejected, whereupon one of Gaynor's law partners went to personally inspect the lists, which Gravesend officials claimed were missing. Gaynor returned to the judge, who now granted the request. When Gaynor's men arrived to enforce the order, they were promptly arrested on charges of drunkenness, vagrancy and disorderly conduct. Popular sentiment was now powerfully against McKane, and Governor Flower went so far as to issue a declaration calling upon election officials to uphold the law. On the day of the election, Republican officials were stationed at the Gravesend polls. McKane had them roughly dispatched and installed his own "Republican" minders. In the end, Gaynor still won the election; in Gravesend, he received 115 votes and his opponent 3,506 (Schieren won as well). For McKane, however, it was the end. Soon afterward, he would be indicted on multiple counts and serve four years (of a six-year sentence) at Sing Sing Prison. Gaynor's reputation, on the other hand, would reach even greater heights. Having exposed and challenged local government corruption, he had gone on to take down one of the most powerful, corrupt and despised of Democratic bosses.

Gaynor took the oath of office on January 2, 1894. As a Supreme Court justice of the Second Judicial District, he heard cases in the counties of Kings, Queens and Richmond (Staten Island), as well as seven others extending in a ninety-mile radius. He soon proved himself to be a highly independent and reasoned judge. Stern but fair, he did not suffer fools and was especially critical of incompetent, arrogant or pompous lawyers. He was particularly respected (if not feared) for his formidable intellect and deep knowledge of the law, particularly its philosophical and historical foundations. He was also remarkably efficient.[155] In 1902, he tried an average of thirty-nine cases per month, while the average for all Brooklyn Supreme Court justices was twenty-three. In the same year, the higher courts affirmed 86 percent of his decisions compared to 68 percent of his colleagues'. As judge, he would also establish a number of legal precedents related to libel and slander, as well as earn respect for his protection of individual rights.

One of the first major cases that Judge Gaynor adjudicated was that brought against Phil Dwyer by the poolroom kingpin Peter De Lacy. Gaynor's formal decision in the matter would be frequently cited for the cogency and solidity of its reasoning (as well as being an excellent example of his concern for individual rights). That June, Gaynor would also become Dwyer's neighbor, moving to number 20 Eighth Avenue. The judge's new home was certainly an upgrade over 212 St. John's and far more fitting for a man of Gaynor's stature (whether the appeal of Sportsmen's Row was a specific attraction is unknown, but it certainly didn't hurt). In addition, proximity to both his close friend Mirabeau Towns (who had moved to number 24 in March 1894) and the Montauk Club (his favored social institution) might have played a role.

Soon after the move, the entire second floor of number 20 became Gaynor's exclusive domain.[156] The larger front room functioned as his library and office, while that in the rear served as his bedroom. The floor was off limits to nearly all, and the Gaynor children would tiptoe past its closed doors so as to not disturb their father at work. Entrance was permitted to only the housemaid and Gaynor's personal secretary, who were tasked with maintaining some sense of organization amid the clutter and myriad documents. It was a Herculean task, as Gaynor was known to eschew the use of a wastebasket, and the floor was constantly littered with papers.

Within number 20, Gaynor's relationship with his wife and children alternated between loving attention and cold indifference, with the occasional bout of anger. Augusta was famed for her beauty and intelligence but most admired for the patience and perseverance she extended her husband. In contrast to Gaynor, she and their six children (four of whom were born in number 20; another died in infancy) were amiable and outgoing. Gaynor's relationship with his children was peculiar; he genuinely enjoyed their company when they were young but seemingly less so by the time they became teenagers. He remained closest with his son Rufus, who, though intelligent, was given to impulsivity. In 1908, for instance, he disappeared from Amherst College mid-semester in order to elope. The Gaynor girls, on the other hand, inherited both their mother's beauty and their father's strong-willed nature. They had no shortage of suitors, but few of them had fortitude enough to contend with their father (two of them, in fact, would later choose to elope). Despite their situation, the girls still managed to be active in the local social scene. Though their curfew was early, they would often sneak out of the roof hatch and onto the roof of number 24, where Towns's sympathetic butler would admit them and provide passage out. When Gaynor discovered the ruse, he had the roof hatch nailed shut.

As time passed, Gaynor spent more and more of his time secluded on the second floor. He took most of his meals and received his many friends there. Of these, perhaps his most frequent caller was Mirabeau Towns. The two shared many common interests, notably literature, as well as their maverick political and legal ideas. They often stayed up late into the night drinking whiskey and immersed in deep conversation about politics and philosophy. Another frequent visitor was Dr. William Morrison,[157] rector of All Saints Episcopal Church where the Gaynor family worshiped (though Gaynor had left the Catholic Church, he never formally committed to another).

Gaynor would serve a fourteen-year term as Supreme Court justice and be reelected to another in 1907. For much of that time, he was repeatedly suggested as a candidate for one office or another, including mayor in

Augusta Gaynor and two of the Gaynor girls in number 20 Eighth Avenue, 1914.

1895 and governor in 1894, 1898, 1901 and 1904. In 1908, he was also briefly considered as William Jenning Bryan's vice-presidential running mate. During the 1894 Democratic convention in Saratoga, rumors began to circulate about Gaynor's previous divorce and his estrangement from the church. Gaynor dispatched Towns to hand deliver a letter to the press requesting that they cease to make an issue of his divorce for the sake of his first wife. Though the papers subsequently ignored the rumors, Gaynor's candidacy lost favor among the delegates; similar rumors also derailed any chance he had with Bryan in 1908.

In 1907, Gaynor was reelected to the bench with the backing of nearly all the relevant political parties and news outlets. This was significant and reflected both the respect he had garnered as a judge and his widespread popularity. Two years later, Gaynor took a stand against police brutality that brought him even further popular acclaim, advocating for a young ne'er-do-well, George Duffy, who was repeatedly harassed by the police though he had never been convicted of any crime. The case generated much press and ultimately resulted in the dismissal of the police commissioner. Having challenged political cronyism and civic corruption and championed personal liberties, Gaynor now took a courageous stand against a police force widely considered to abuse its powers.

By the summer of 1909, there was a palpable sense that now was the time for Gaynor to seek the mayoralty. He was attractive to both the Democrats and Republicans and had the enthusiastic support of Joseph Pulitzer and his *New York World* and the tacit backing of William Randolph Hearst, owner of the rival *New York Journal*. Pulitzer even went so far as to instruct his editors to "urge vigorously Gaynor's nomination by Democrats. Admitting his defects, he is an able man; nobody's pocket judge."[158] That Gaynor was nobody's "pocket judge," however, remained a concern to the major political parties. Though his independence made him something of a risk, he was nevertheless exceedingly popular and eminently electable. He had already received the endorsement of some fifty reform-minded groups.

In the end, it was Tammany Hall that chose to nominate him. Its leader, Charles Francis Murphy—who had inherited the mantle from Richard Croker after the latter had gone off to race in England with Mike Dwyer—chose to back the most electable candidate and the one who might also provide an embattled Tammany some legitimacy. Though it went against his reformist credentials, Gaynor accepted the nomination, believing that Tammany afforded him the best chance to win. It was a strange alliance, the chief of bosses and the boss-buster, but politics does truly make for strange bedfellows. On the day that the Tammany Democrats came to his house to officially nominate him, Gaynor kept them waiting in the living room for hours while he tinkered with his acceptance speech in his upstairs suite.

Gaynor's campaign was unorthodox, to say the least. He initially forewent a campaign manager and conducted his campaign from the living room and office of number 20. He also refused any donations, returning the first two checks he received: $1,000 from Abraham Abraham and $500 from Schuyler Parsons, president of the Coney Island Jockey Club.[159] By accepting Tammany's backing, however, Gaynor lost the support of the reform-minded Hearst (somewhat hypocritically, as Hearst had previously served a term in Congress with Tammany's support, but again, strange bedfellows). A bitter rivalry subsequently developed, with an angry war of words fought on the pages of the *New York Journal* and on the campaign trail. William Ivins, a lawyer and putative Hearst spokesperson, led the attack. Many of the charges were rehashes of old (his divorce, estrangement from Catholicism, his temper), but there were also new questions about Gaynor's relationship with horse racing. Ivins charged that Gaynor had conspired with racing interests to use his judgeship to nullify recent anti-gambling legislation. The evidence? Gaynor's mortgage on the Brighton track and his friendship with the younger Engeman.[160] Though the 1894 case against Dwyer apparently escaped Ivins's notice (as did the symbolism of his residence on Sportsmen's Row), Gaynor's association with the sport and its leading figures was sufficient enough to lend the charge some credibility.

In 1909, Gaynor ran on two major platforms: municipal ownership of the subway system and a crackdown on police abuse. He maintained his popular appeal, but his acid tongue helped him lose the support of all but two of New York's twelve major papers (though one was Pulitzer's *New York World*, which had the largest circulation). On the campaign trail, his caustic nature was readily apparent to the voters, but his intellectualism, atypical character and peculiar campaign earned him admirers, particularly among the city's minorities. At a campaign stop on the Lower Eastside, for instance, he offered that it was unfair that the Jews be forced to also close their shops on Sunday, as their Sabbath fell on Saturday (noting that the law merely required observation of a Sabbath and not which one). Needless to say, it was a well-received declaration.

On election day, Gaynor received some 43 percent of the vote, earning him a clear majority and the mayoralty (Hearst, who had also entered

William Gaynor departing number 20 Eighth Avenue.

the multi-candidate race, garnered 27 percent). The Tammany ticket was otherwise a flop, with all its other candidates defeated. That evening, the press gathered in the living room of number 20 waiting for Gaynor to address them. The mayor-elect, however, remained in seclusion with his friends on the second floor. He eventually sent down the Reverend Dr. Morrison with a simple note: "I have nothing to say, except to present my compliments to the newspaper proprietors and editors."[161] It had been a brutal, ugly fight.

On his first day in office, January 1, 1910, Gaynor walked from his house on Eighth Avenue to City Hall in downtown Manhattan via the Brooklyn Bridge. It was the first time he had ever been to the seat of New York City's government. To the assembled crowd, he offered a brief inaugural address: "I enter upon this office with the intention of doing the very best I can for the City of New York. That will have to suffice; I can do no more."[162] That night, he walked back home.

Attempted assassination of Mayor Gaynor, August 10, 1910. *Photograph by William Warnecke, New York World.*

The Mayor

In June 1910, two elegant "mayor's lamps" were placed on the pillars that flanked the stoop of number 20. This was an old custom (tradition held as far back as the Dutch) meant to announce the significance of the residence.[163] The lamps were quite distinct, consisting of ornate sconces set on ornamental bases and topped with eagles. By 1910, these had been electrified.

Mayor's lamps aside, Gaynor soon proved himself anything but traditional and, to Tammany's horror, no pocket politician either. He appointed almost exclusively independent deputies and began ferreting out and eliminating no-show positions. Brought to power by Tammany, he was now systematically dismantling its network of municipal patronage. He also instituted widespread fiscal reforms aimed at eliminating waste and redundancy. The transformation of municipal governance was so earnest and rapid that almost all of the papers—with the notable exception of Hearst's *New York Journal*, with whom Gaynor's rivalry grew even nastier—became strikingly positive in their reporting on the mayor's efforts.

The first seven months of Gaynor's term were the culmination of his professional career, a virtual *quinquennium Neronis* in which he had become, in every sense of the word, a true statesman. Though his steely exterior remained intact, his efforts (and successes) betrayed a remarkable acumen for the demands of the office. And so, seeking a break from his almost nonstop work, he set out for Europe with Rufus on August 9, 1910. Soon after boarding the *Kaiser Wilhelm der Grosse* at Hoboken, Gaynor was approached by a man lurking in the background and shot through the neck at point-blank range. The incident was captured by William Warnecke, a *New York World* photographer, and remains one of the most dramatic moments in photojournalism ever documented. Soon afterward, the gunman was restrained by William "Big Bill" Edwards, street cleaning commissioner (and former Princeton footballer).

The would-be assassin, James J. Gallagher, had been recently fired from his work at the docks. Mentally ill, he believed that Gaynor was the cause of his troubles. The mayor was taken to St. Mary's Hospital in Hoboken, where he stayed for three weeks. After further convalescence at his Long Island summer home, he returned to work on October 3, where some ten thousand well-wishers gathered to greet him. In the two months between the assassination attempt and his return to work, Gaynor had come to national attention, earning plaudits for his leadership and respect for the stoicism with which he handled the calamity.

Though Gaynor had survived the attempt, the incident left him both physically and emotionally scarred. The bullet could not be removed, and its presence ("this fishhook," as he called it) made his voice hoarse and gave rise to a chronic cough. The impact on his psyche, however, was far more consequential. He became increasingly impatient, and his temper—which had always been ferocious—he was now unable to control. It was a volatile mixture. The pressing issues that the city faced, particularly the subway contracts and the institution of a new municipal charter, required compromise and conciliation, attributes never strong in Gaynor and now seemingly absent. Gaynor handled both quite clumsily, prevaricating over municipal ownership (of which he had run in favor) and presenting an unpopular charter that gave the mayor enhanced power and authority. Though the populace still largely supported him, he soon lost the support of the newspapers and reformers, both hard-won allies. And then, in 1912, a police scandal came to light that reflected poorly on the mayor and his handpicked police commissioner: a sensational murder ordered by a crooked police lieutenant.

In 1913, Gaynor stood for reelection as an independent. The stresses of the previous few years had taken their toll, and the mayor had grown quite frail. The upcoming campaign promised to be arduous, so he and Rufus planned a brief vacation. On September 5, they boarded the *Baltic*, intending to sail roundtrip to England. Gaynor spent much of his time reading and finding the relaxation that he so desperately required. His health seemed to be improving, but this proved only illusory. On September 12, Rufus found his body slumped over in his deck chair, dead; just ten minutes before, he had placed his order for lunch.

Upon arrival in Liverpool, Gaynor's body was transferred to the ill-starred *Lusitania* for the trip home. Arriving in New York on September 19, the corpse was transferred without fanfare to his home on Eighth Avenue. There, on September 20, a small service for family and friends was held while the honorary pallbearers, including former president Howard Taft, waited in the Montauk Club across the street. When the service concluded, Gaynor's casket was removed from number 20 and carried down Eighth Avenue, escorted by two hundred mounted policemen. Crowds thronged the street, and all of the residents of Sportsmen's Row solemnly gathered on their stoops to watch the mayor's last trip to city hall. The cavalcade proceeded down Flatbush Avenue and across the Brooklyn Bridge, with thousands of mourners lining the route. In the rotunda of City Hall, Gaynor's body lay in state for a day before being conveyed back across the bridge to Green-Wood

Two policemen stand guard before number 20 Eighth Avenue, September 20, 1913. Note the mayoral lamps on the pillars flanking the stoop. *Courtesy of Library of Congress, Prints & Photographs Division, LC-DIG-ggbain-14299.*

Waiting for the private funeral ceremony to conclude, September 20, 1913. *Courtesy of Library of Congress, Prints & Photographs Division, LC-DIG-ggbain-14302.*

Gaynor's coffin being removed from number 20, September 20, 1913. *Courtesy of Library of Congress, Prints & Photographs Division, LC-DIG-ggbain-14300.*

Mayor Gaynor's funeral procession along Sportsmen's Row, view to the north. Photograph taken from the steps of the Montauk Club. *Courtesy of Brown Brothers.*

Mayor Gaynor's funeral procession along Sportsmen's Row, view to the south. Number 26 Eighth Avenue is to the right. Photograph taken from the steps of the Montauk Club. *Courtesy of Brown Brothers.*

Cemetery, where the mayor was laid to rest. Again, thousands came out to pay their final respects. Though estranged from the press and the mainstream parties, Gaynor died very much a man beloved by and of the people.

With Gaynor's passing, the block lost its most prominent resident. Its most significant denizen, however, was not an individual but an institution.

THE MONTAUK CLUB

The Big Neighbor to the East

During the saga of Spite Row, Edward Dodge had lambasted the Montauk Club as Sportsmen's Row's "stingy, if not mean, big neighbor." Dodge's frustration with the club was understandable, but his castigation was only partially correct. Stingy? Perhaps. Mean? No. Big? Yes. Certainly the club's history and that of Sportsmen's Row were intimately tied in the 1890s and early 1900s. The club, after all, dominated the eastern side of the block. More significantly, the club's presence conferred the ultimate prestige on Sportsmen's Row. Soon after its founding, it became the premier social institution of the city.

Brooklyn's remarkable growth during the 1880s and 1890s had ushered an expansion of social organizations to meet the needs of its burgeoning elite society. New clubs were established, while a number of older organizations constructed new, more extravagant headquarters (such as Carl Goepel's 1890 efforts for the Germania Club). The first social club established on the park slope was the Carleton Club, founded in 1881. Its clubhouse was located at the corner of Sixth and St. Mark's Avenues (where a subsequent edifice, dating to 1890, still stands). As development expanded toward Prospect Park, there was rising interest in establishing another club farther up the hill.[164] To this end, twenty-five interested residents met at the home of Norton Q. Pope on December 13, 1888 (located at 241 Park Place, and since demolished; notably, Mrs. Pope owned one of the most important collections of incunabula and early Elizabethan books in the world). Other meetings soon followed, at which several possible names for the new organization were

The Montauk Club, circa 1900, from Plaza Street looking west. Number 24 Eighth Avenue is visible to the left. *Collection of the New York Historical Society.*

Breaking ground for the Montauk Club, October 2, 1889. *Courtesy of the Brooklyn Historical Society.*

bandied about, including the Seatalcot, Prospect, Prospect Park, Crystal and Constellation. Eventually, the name Montauk was decided upon, invoking the tribe that was believed to have once been the most powerful of Long Island. The editors of the *Brooklyn Daily Eagle* also liked that the native word supposedly meant "hilly" or "high land."[165] On March 11, 1889, the group, now totaling some three hundred subscribers, signed the club's certificate of incorporation. Later that month, the nascent organization rented 34 Eighth Avenue for use as a temporary clubhouse; it was here that Mayor Chapin's move to Sportsmen's Row was celebrated on May 16, 1889.

The club's first order of business was the erection of a permanent headquarters in the immediate vicinity. In late March, it purchased a 117- by 110-foot plot on the southeast corner of Eighth Avenue and Lincoln Place for $40,000.[166] With its commanding views across Grand Army Plaza and the park beyond, it was an ideal location. Ground was broken on October 2, and the building's cornerstone was laid on December 14. At three o'clock that afternoon, in a driving snow and sleet, an overflowing crowd assembled beneath an awning while others huddled nearby under their umbrellas. After an invocation by the Reverend George F. Breed of St. John's Episcopal Church, finance committee chairman (and future mayor) David Boody took to the podium to address the crowd. He spoke of Brooklyn's prosperity, the spirit of its citizens and the significance of its social clubs:[167]

We meet here today to lay the cornerstone of an institution that marks the growth and prosperity of our city and the public spirit of our citizens...Every institution such as the one upon whose foundations we now stand strengthens the sentiment of local attachment...These clubs, then, not only speak of civic prosperity, they indicate a growing sentiment of fraternity, a sentiment that will yet bear rich fruit in the way of works of public usefulness and adornment.

When he finished, the crowd broke into ebullient applause. Next, General Stewart L. Woodford, who had first suggested the name Montauk, came forward and sketched a brief history of the tribe. Following, club president Charles A. Moore, with an ivory-handled silver trowel in hand, ceremonially laid the building's cornerstone: a five-foot-square block of Ohio Freestone inscribed "1889." A copper hollow within held a copy of the Constitution; a list of federal, state and city officials; and copies of the day's papers. After a concluding prayer by Thomas A. Nelson of the Memorial Presbyterian Church, the group retired to number 34 to celebrate.

The club spared no expense in building its clubhouse. An earlier design competition had been won by Francis Kimball (1845–1919), who had previously designed a number of houses and churches and had also assisted William Burges in the construction of Trinity College in Hartford, Connecticut. Kimball was deeply influenced by John Ruskin's *Stones of Venice* (1851), and the headquarters he designed for the club was a masterwork of the Venetian Gothic style that evokes the great palazzi of Venice, particularly the Ca D'Oro.

The Montauk clubhouse stands four stories, plus a basement and attic.[168] Constructed of multi-toned bricks of brown, orange and red and highlighted with brownstone and terracotta revetments, the whole ensemble is cleverly balanced and radiates a warm, golden hue. Three of its sides are extensively adorned: that along Eighth Avenue (where its main entrance is located), Lincoln Place and Plaza Street. The north side—facing onto the parcel of land upon which the houses of Spite Row would later be built—was left unadorned, the thought being that the club would eventually expand.

Each of the three decorated sides is unique in appearance. The Eighth Avenue façade is asymmetrical at its bottom two stories, with a massed bay and loggia to the right of the main entrance, while the window arrangement of the upper two floors are balanced and symmetrical. The main entrance is reached by a high stoop, with a line of carved Indian heads above the door. Above this is a round arched window, capped with a terracotta frieze that portrays the laying of the building's cornerstone; this latter panel

Detail, the Montauk Club. Photo by Dinanda Nooney. *Courtesy of Photography Collection, Miriam and Ira D. Wallach Division of Arts, Prints and Photographs, New York Public Library.*

Bowling alley of the Montauk Club (1978). Photo by Dinanda Nooney. *Courtesy of Photography Collection, Miriam and Ira D. Wallach Division of Arts, Prints and Photographs, New York Public Library.*

caused a "great tizzy-wizzy" at the time for its poorly proportioned—or, more accurately, overly portly—figures, which *Brooklyn Life* described as a "grotesque piece of imagery."[169] To the left, and reached by a smaller stoop, is the ladies' entrance. This permitted women to access the upper floors without entering the main lobby. The Lincoln Place side consists of a large and gently curving bay on the bottom floor, with a balustrade above. On that facing Plaza Street is a two-story bay, also curving and carrying a balcony above. Around all three sides on the third story runs a continuous frieze that depicts various scenes of the Montauk Indians; at one time, there was a balcony above this (since removed). Architectural details on all sides include quatrefoils, dwarf columns and traceried fenestrations. The roof is a playful composition of high chimneys crowned with American eagles and steep gables of red terracotta tile. The builder was Charles T. Wilson, the foremost contractor in metropolitan New York, and the outstanding preservation of the building owes much to the quality with which it was originally constructed.

The club's first floor contained a large reception room and reading room. The second story consisted of two large billiard rooms, two small card rooms and a boardroom. The grand dining room was located on the third floor, as were the ladies' reception and dining rooms. Six apartments, a large communal bathroom and the so-called Jolly Room (a shared lounge facing Plaza Street, with adjoining balcony) composed the fourth, while an attic above contained servants' quarters. A bowling alley, coatroom and bathroom were located in the basement. In all, the building cost $162,686 and its furnishings $29,586 (including the $40,000 spent to acquire the land, the entire club cost some $232,272).[170] The bulk of the cost was covered by a sale of $150,000 in bonds. The club took possession of the clubhouse on May 1, 1891, and hosted a gala opening on May 23, though final work on interior carpentry and exterior masonry were not completed until later that year.[171]

With its inviting interior and wealth of amenities, the Montauk Club provided a place of refuge and fellowship for its members. It also offered them a robust social calendar, with lectures, musical performances and holiday celebrations filling out the year. The club also played an important role in a number of civic affairs, most significantly hosting the luncheon for the marshal and dignitaries for Brooklyn's annual Anniversary Day parade.[172] The club became famous, however, for its extravagant dinner parties. These were large, elegant and nationally known affairs that honored and feted the leading men of the age. Over the years, these included all of Brooklyn's mayors; Mayor Gaynor (also a member); various congressmen and senators; and, most notably, by 1920 four eventual presidents (Grover Cleveland, William McKinley, William Taft and Calvin Coolidge). Cleveland had been a guest on October 21, 1892, just a few years after the hope that he might consider a move to number 27 Eighth Avenue. Other honorees included Admiral Robert Peary (first to the North Pole, or so he claimed), Samuel Clemens, Calvert Vaux and St. Clair McKelway, editor of the *Brooklyn Daily Eagle* (who had earlier brought Gaynor to the attention of the *Brooklyn Argus*). During the Spanish-American and First World Wars, a number of military officials were guests, including Rear Admiral William T. Sampson, the commanding officers of the various battleships at the Battle of Santiago and General Horace Porter (secretary to Ulysses S. Grant).

Of all the club's famous guests, perhaps none was more celebrated by contemporaries than Chauncey Mitchell Depew (April 23, 1834–April 5, 1928). An attorney by trade, Depew met with success in both railroading and local politics, culminating in the presidency of the New York Central Railroad (1885–98) and as United States senator (1899–1911). He was also a talented and versatile orator.[173] On April 23, 1892, he was invited to speak at the club on the occasion of his fifty-eighth birthday. His speech was so well received that he was given an honorary membership and an invitation to return for his birthday in the following year.[174]

His address in the following year, however, wasn't nearly as well received. He began by extolling Brooklyn's virtues but soon veered into a condemnation of its corrupt government:[175]

> *Self-government in cities is on trial, and Brooklyn should, as Brooklyn can, be in the front of well-governed cities. The men here tonight can rescue Brooklyn from the outlaws who are in possession of her government, and make her an example of high purposes in official life and success in good government.*

Sitting in the crowd was club member David Boody, then mayor of Brooklyn, who was already under fire from the reform efforts of Gaynor and Ziegler. At the conclusion of the speech, Boody stormed off. The awkward incident dominated the headlines for several days, and the mayor's sudden departure was taken by some as a tacit admission of guilt. The *Brooklyn Daily Eagle* managed to solicit comment from Gaynor, who offered, "I would prefer to say nothing about it. I was not at the dinner. It is very evident that Mr. Depew spoke deliberately."[176]

The uproar soon subsided, and Depew was invited back to the club for his birthday in 1894. Thenceforth, he returned annually to celebrate his birthday and opine on all matters political, economic and social. With advancing age, he also became increasingly more philosophical and contemplative. As he offered in his 1899 address:[177]

> *My friends, we pass this way but once. We cannot retrace our steps to any preceding milestone. Every time the clock strikes, it is both the announcement of the hour upon which we are entering and the knell of the one which is gone.*

Introspection aside, Depew's annual visit remained a highly anticipated and celebratory occasion. All told, he delivered thirty-four birthday speeches, missing only once (1906), and giving his final address in 1926 at the age of ninety-two.

JAMES AND THOMAS H. TROY, NUMBER 26 EIGHTH AVENUE

From 1889 through 1931, the Montauk Club had only four presidents: Charles A. Moore (1889–1901), Thomas H. Troy (1901–04), Timothy Woodruff (1904–08) and William H. English (1908–31). All were effective and popular presidents, and the relative continuity of leadership was of great benefit to the club.

Moore had been a particularly effective leader, but professional commitments required him to move to Manhattan and resign his position in the fall of 1901. On December 2, Thomas H. Troy was unanimously elected to succeed him. If Sportsmen's Row felt that the club had failed it in its struggle with Peterson and Spite Row, it could no longer claim a disconnected leadership. Troy resided at number 26 Eighth Avenue, which he and his father, James Troy, had purchased from Mike Dwyer in April 1893.

James Troy was born in Ireland in 1836.[178] After immigrating to the United States, he settled in Brooklyn and took up the study and practice of law, gaining admission to the bar in 1856. His legal competence and versatility brought him much attention, and he was appointed assistant district attorney of Kings County (1862–67) and subsequently elected county judge for King's County, a position he held until 1870. A marriage produced one son, Thomas Henry (b. 1860), with whom the elder Troy was quite close. His son followed him in the study of law, and the two established a practice in Brooklyn Heights in the late 1870s.

After James Troy's wife, Elizabeth, died at the family's home (71 First Place) on December 23, 1892, following a long illness,[179] the Troys moved to Eighth Avenue that spring. In the following year, James Troy took on his most famous client: John McKane, the boss of Gravesend, whose downfall Gaynor—now also Troy's neighbor—had so skillfully engineered (as if the courtroom interaction among the residents of Sportsmen's Row wasn't already frequent enough, Robert H. Furey, son of William and nephew of Robert, was McKane's bondsman).[180]

Before joining his father in practice, Thomas Troy attended the Polytechnic Institute of Brooklyn,[181] of which he later became a trustee. He married Emily Turner in June 1891, but the union produced no children. The couple continued to reside with the groom's parents and moved with Judge Troy to Sportsmen's Row following Elizabeth's passing. Immediately following their move, the Troys became members of the club. When Thomas was elected to complete Moore's unfinished term, he was chairman of its all-important Entertainment Committee.

Troy's election came only a few months after the completion of Spite Row. Moore seems to have escaped any personal reproach for his failure to stop their completion—that fell more generally on the board of directors—but it was impossible for Troy to turn back the clock. Though Dodge had departed, Sportsmen's Row's other residents remained, and those who belonged to the club continued their membership (Dodge discontinued his). Troy soon proved a worthy successor to Moore. The club's annual report in March 1891 noted that the club had 441 members: 400 residents, 16 nonresidents, 20 honorary and 5 life members, and assets of $262,397.48 against liabilities of $236,966.56, leaving a surplus of $25,430.92.[182] By every measure, this was an improvement over the club's performance in previous years. Not surprisingly, Troy was unanimously elected to another term in April 1902. In his second term, he oversaw the formation of a local civic group, which sought to advocate and lobby for the neighborhood. While nothing substantive came of its work, the group did make it clear that it preferred the name Prospect Heights to Park Slope.[183] Troy did not stand for reelection in 1904, and the presidency went to Timothy Woodruff, former lieutenant governor of the state and resident of 94 Eighth Avenue.

For his service to the club, Troy was honored with a dinner on March 11, 1905, and given a $500 watch inscribed *laudat, tentat, vincit* ("he praises, he strives, he overcomes").[184]

The Troys continued their successful legal practice well into the new century. James, even at an advanced age, remained particularly respected and affectionately known as the "Dean of the Brooklyn Bar." He worked, in fact, right up until his death from pleurisy at the age of eighty-two.[185] He died on Monday, January 8, 1917, at home, and his funeral—like that of so many of Sportsmen's Row's residents—was held at the Church of St. Augustine that Thursday. In October of that year, Thomas Troy put the contents of number 26, a "palatial residence," up for auction.[186] Among the items noted were three thousand books, valuable oil paintings and a thirteen-piece Belter parlor set. Also mentioned were a set of mounted tiger, leopard, polar bear and lion skins, as well as an assortment of moose and elk heads. Needless to say, modern sensibilities might have found the Troy home somewhat stuffy, if not downright macabre (though thoroughly Victorian). By 1920, Troy and his wife had departed for the Hotel Bossert, rejoining their former neighbors Carl and Mathilde Goepel. Troy died of cardiac failure on December 14, 1928, and was laid to rest, without a burial marker, in Green-Wood Cemetery.

MEMBER-RESIDENTS OF SPORTSMEN'S ROW

From its inception, the club's membership comprised a virtual who's who of Brooklyn's elite. Among its notable early members were William Ziegler, Frederick and Charles M. Pratt (sons of the oil magnate and founder of Brooklyn's Pratt Institute), Leonard Moody (Brooklyn's real estate king), J. Rogers Maxwell, Charles Feltman, John Hanan, Edward H. Litchfield (son of Edwin Litchfield, the largest landowner in Brooklyn whose mansion still stands in Prospect Park) and Mayors Chapin, Boody and Schieren. Though men of standing, each would have undergone the club's whimsical initiation rite: with their heads crowned in a mantle of eagle feathers and their faces decorated with war paint, the members would surround them and chant, "Wah, hoo, wah."[187]

Absent on any surviving membership directory of the club, however, are the names Dwyer, Garrison or Rowe (not that Mike Dwyer, given his domestic predilection, would have had any interest in belonging). Article XIII of the club's bylaws banned gambling, which—given its centrality to the sport—may have been something of a deterrent. The prohibition, however, does suggest one significant barrier: social class. Horse racing may have been the sport of kings, but the celebrity of its pigskin knights did not necessarily equate to social standing. Garrison's exploits made for popular entertainment, not polite dinner conversation. In this regard, one cannot help but recall that one of the complaints about Julian Ralph's 1892 travel guide to Brooklyn was that he had associated the likes of a Garrison and McLaughlin with a respectable, self-made industrialist such as Thomas Adams Jr. (who became a member in 1889).

The majority of Sportsmen's Row's other residents, however, were at one time or another members of the club. This was particularly true by the dawn of the new century, when the block was dominated by the "right" type of client—i.e. lawyers and politicians. In the 1900–01 conflict with Peterson, for instance, the head of almost every household belonged. Member residents of Sportsmen's Row (and the year in which they joined) include: Gaynor (1889), Williams (1889), Goepel (1891), Dodge (1892), Towns (1892), the Troys (1893), Hyde (1900), Robert Furey (1900) and John Furey (1907). Among those closely associated with Sportsmen's Row, Pinkerton (1889), the younger Engeman (1889) and Shevlin (1900) also belonged. Engeman and Shevlin, though deeply involved in horse racing, were well educated and ran in elite circles and their primary livelihoods lay elsewhere (though if owning a racetrack didn't always cut it, owning a baseball team could: both Edward [Ed] McKeever and his brother Stephen were members. The two had purchased half of the Brooklyn Dodgers in 1912 and, along with principal owner Charles Ebbets, built Ebbets Field in 1912–13).

The club's presence on Sportsmen's Row made it a conspicuous part of its physical fabric, and the involvement of many of its residents ensured that it played an active role in their lives. It was also a factor in two of the block's most compelling stories: the struggle against Peterson and Robert Furey's estrangement from his brother and subsequent retirement to the club's fourth floor. Gaynor's association with the club was particularly profound (and its proximity may have been a factor in his move to number 20). He was honored by the club on several occasions, and it later played host to his mayoral transitional meetings in 1912. The affiliation also played a role in one of the most significant events in the history of New York City: its 1898 consolidation. In December 1892, Gaynor gave an inspiring speech at the club that spurred a disparate block of leading citizens and professionals to form the Brooklyn Consolidation League (BCL), with the goal of uniting the two cities.[188] The group was seeking to address the insurmountable problems faced by Brooklyn: a small revenue base increasingly unable to support the infrastructure necessary to meet the needs of its population. Gaynor's speech, and his subsequent work with the BCL, helped bring about the merger in 1898.

The Montauk Club, however, was not the only club originally associated with the block.

The Late, Great Brooklyn Riding and Driving Club

At the time the Montauk Club was being conceived, plans were also afoot to establish an entirely different type of social institution in Brooklyn, to be focused exclusively on equestrian sports. Such organizations were a phenomenon of the same milieu that fostered the rise of mass entertainment (such as Coney Island) and the professionalization of sports: leisure time borne of the industrial revolution. Unlike these more plebian diversions, however, urban equestrianism was almost exclusively an aristocratic pursuit. While New York City possessed several such clubs, Brooklyn had none of any note.

In the spring of 1889, thirty of Brooklyn's leading men set about to redress this deficiency by establishing a club near the ample bridle paths and open spaces of Prospect Park while also being far removed from the noise and filth of the elevated and steam railroads.[189] The group was fortunate to find a leader in the forty-five-year-old Albert H. Smith, a charismatic young banker of the firm Mills, Robeson and Smith. Smith poured himself into the endeavor, striving to make it as successful as possible. He consulted with numerous architects and visited the equestrian clubs of various cities, collecting information regarding their clubhouses and organizations.

That June, the group was able to purchase a large parcel of land to the west of Grand Army Plaza—and just across Flatbush Avenue from Sportsmen's Row. On the nineteenth of the month, the Brooklyn Riding and Driving Club was formally incorporated, stating its objective as the "cultivation of social relations among its members and the development of athletic sports, including riding and driving."[190] Soon thereafter, the fledgling club retained the services of the esteemed architectural firm of McKim, Mead and White to design its clubhouse.[191]

At McKim, Mead and White, it fell to Sidney Stratton (August 8, 1845–June 17, 1921), a long-standing partner of the firm, to design the actual building. The structure that came to life at his drafting table—and that would ultimately be erected—was deeply inspired by the architecture of imperial Rome. Though the legacy of Rome was readily apparent throughout the McKim, Mead and White oeuvre, the antecedents of the Brooklyn Riding and Driving Club were to be found in its more utilitarian architecture—the stark yet imposing simplicity of its military fortifications, aqueducts and *basilicae*. Here, Stratton would cleverly evoke that most equestrian of Roman structures: the circus. It would also prove to be Stratton's last major commission.

The club was situated on a four-acre site, shaped like an irregular triangle, bordered by Vanderbilt Avenue and Plaza and Butler Streets (Butler is now Sterling Place). It consisted of a complex of three interconnected buildings: a clubhouse, riding ring and stables. The monumental façade of the clubhouse, 104 feet long by 30 feet deep, stood on the west side of Vanderbilt

Façade and clubhouse, Brooklyn Riding and Driving Club. *Courtesy of the Brooklyn Historical Society.*

Lounge, Brooklyn Riding and Driving Club. *Courtesy of the Brooklyn Historical Society.*

Avenue.[192] It was three stories tall and sat atop a semi-sunken basement. Three monumental arches reached to the second story, flanked on either side by two tower-like structures, each topped with a one-story colonnaded pavilion. These skillfully evoked the towers that traditionally flanked the *carceres*, or starting gates, of a Roman circus. The building's main entrances were located in the two outer arches of the façade, with the northern (i.e., to the right, looking head-on) designated for women and the men's to the south. The interior contained a suite of spaces, including lounges, dressing rooms, offices and a glassed-in viewing gallery that overlooked the adjacent riding ring. The whole interior was finished with carved mahogany, primavera and other decorative hardwoods.

The grand riding hall, the main feature of the club, measured roughly 180 by 100 feet.[193] At the time of its completion, it was the largest private indoor riding ring in the country. The hall contained a narrow seating promenade, thirty-three box seats, a balcony for musicians and a tanbark floor. By day, the hall was well lit by its monumental arched windows

Brooklyn Riding and Driving Club, lounge overlooking the riding ring. *Courtesy of the Brooklyn Historical Society.*

and at night with electrical lights. A triangle-shaped mounting paddock was situated on the Plaza Street side in the space created by the curve of Plaza Street away from the building's axis. Adjacent to the riding hall were the stables, housed in a three-story pavilion that referenced and counterbalanced the monumental clubhouse. This contained stalls for two hundred horses, a blacksmith's shop and storage for carriages and riding equipment. The structure was interconnected by a series of ramps and had exits to both Plaza and Butler Streets.

The entire complex was constructed of Roman-style brick that, speckled with iron, provided a visually pleasing counterbalance to the lush greenery of the park and the berms that ran parallel to Plaza Street. Although somewhat busy, the entire structure was effectively held together by the unifying succession of arches. At its completion, the exterior would be remarkably faithful to Stratton's original vision, save a monumental bronze statue of horses intended for the clubhouse façade fronting Vanderbilt Avenue.

Stable interior, Brooklyn Riding and Driving Club. *Courtesy of the Brooklyn Historical Society.*

By the fall of 1890, construction was well underway, and Smith was the toast of local society. His arrest for forgery that November was therefore greeted with shock and surprise.[194] An agent at Mills, Robeson and Smith had discovered that Smith had been crudely doctoring stock certificates, adding zeroes to the share amounts. The company had borrowed heavily against the falsified shares, and Smith had siphoned the money into his personal account. The firm, some $360,000 in arrears, was ruined. That December, Smith was sentenced to seventeen years at Sing Sing.[195]

From the fall of 1890 through early 1891, the club's complex opened in piecemeal fashion. In November 1891, the structure was sufficiently complete to host a communal Thanksgiving, with riding and hurdle jumping forming the focus of the festivities. The interior of the clubhouse took somewhat longer to finish, and its final details were not installed until the end of the year.

When completed, the club offered a range of services. It retained experts in all matters equestrian and offered private instruction and weekly classes and provided storage for members' horses, buggies and apparatus. An article from the April 6, 1896 *New York Times* provides a window into the types of equestrian activities it provided:

> *Nearly every morning, afternoon, and evening of the week the ring is occupied by a class either of ladies, gentlemen, or young people. The ladies class meets twice a week in the morning, the mounted athletic association drills Tuesday nights, Col. Partridge's class rides Friday evenings, the ladies tandem class is instructed two afternoons a week, and Wednesday evenings and Saturday afternoons there are general music rides.*

The club also mounted a good number of equestrian competitions, such as tent-pegging and pumpkin racing, which, though chimerical in title, were quite militaristic in nature. Tent pegging, for instance, required the rider to spear an object at high-speed and carry it some distance. There was also the *jeu de barre* contest for women, in which the object was to capture the ribbons attached to the left shoulder of each rider without losing one's own. These were held to great fanfare two to three times per year, and the winner received a silver Tiffany cup.

From its inception, the club had taken a particular interest in its potential and appeal to women. They were permitted membership in the club when there was no male head of the house, and—though they were not able to sit on the board—their participation in the club's activities and social life easily matched that of the men. In part, the club provided a respectable outlet in which to engage in activities normally outside the realm of accepted social norms, so activities such as rough riding and *jeu de barre* found both willing participants and, it should be noted, willing spectators of both sexes.

Beginning in 1893, the club hosted an annual horseshow. Its original purpose was to showcase the quality of the members' horses and horsemanship, as well as celebrate the club's phenomenal success.[196] That first show, a four-day affair, opened on the evening of Wednesday, April 12. Almost a third of the club's members, including twenty women, entered 120 horses for fifty-three different contests. The event brought out the very best of Brooklyn society, "the Brooklyn belles in bewitching costumes, and Brooklyn youth resplendent in drab coats, riding breeches, boots, and glossy bell-topped hats, with the curliest of brims."[197] Over the course of the show's four evenings, thousands of spectators jammed the clubhouse, which was at standing room only. To carefully selected music, friends and family watched their loved ones compete in a range of categories, including (in the parlance of the day) trotters, roadsters, horses in harness, carriage horses, tandems, four in hand teams, ponies on harness, saddle horses, ponies under saddle, hunters and jumping classes. Finally, as with any proper Victorian affair, there was a novelty class with such categories as smallest pony under saddle and most attractive horse older than fifteen years (the crowd held much admiration for one remarkable twenty-five-year-old entry).

In a world reliant on the horse for labor, movement and recreation, the show captured the attention of the city, and all of the newspapers, including those in neighboring New York City, were in admiration of the club's efforts. It ranked, instantly, among the top equestrian events of the region. It also made a legend of club member Frank Beard, who dominated the competition, winning in nineteen different events. For all of the praise the show garnered, however, one reporter couldn't help but note that, for all of the quality and diversity of horse shown, one class was noticeably absent: Thoroughbreds. And, as he went on, this was all the more striking considering that one of the greatest owners of Thoroughbreds was a Brooklyn man: Mike Dwyer.[198] Ironically, Mike Dwyer was also literally next door—just down the block on Eighth Avenue. Even if the show had been of interest, Dwyer's thoughts lay elsewhere. This was the very same month that he was departing Sportsmen's Row for New York City following the death of his wife.

Given the success and attention of the first show, it subsequently became a regular feature of the club, held every year in the spring. Over time, it also became increasingly more sophisticated and professionalized. In 1894, several of the classes were opened to non-members, and by the following year the show had begun to attract competitors from outside the area. More competition classes were added, and the number of overall entries subsequently increased. The selection of judges also became increasingly important. In 1894, for instance, the eight judges included Frank K. Sturgis, steward of the Jockey Club, and Samuel W. Taylor, editor of *Rider and Driver* magazine.

By the early years of the twentieth century, the annual horseshow had become a colorful mix of professional and amateur equestrianism. Lillian Hyde rode in 1910, while the 1913 show featured performances by Ruth Gaynor, the youngest daughter of Mayor Gaynor, as well as by William H. Moore, a renowned international horseman. By the 1920s, the competition categories were tweaked to reflect the changing times: harness classes were dropped, added and dropped again, while Polo ponies, of increasing interest to the club, were added. The 1926 Thirty-fourth Annual Show was the undoubted pinnacle:[199] over one thousand entries, with a full slate of professional and amateur events, and prizes including a $1,500 gold cup provided by the Leeming family. It also featured Colonel Theodore Roosevelt on a blue-ribbon panel of judges. The highlight of the show, however, was an appearance by popular New York City mayor Jimmy Walker, who entered his horse Cedar King in the saddle competitions. Though Cedar King wasn't a winner, the mayor was awarded, to uproarious applause, a blue rosette by the club for "being the best mayor New York ever had." At the show's conclusion, the mayor leapt from the judges' stand into the carriage of Mrs. Edward B. Quinn, with whom he circled the riding hall before exiting to the exaltation of the audience.

For all of Smith's careful planning, the phenomenal success of the club's earliest years exposed some shortcomings in its original configuration and design. These included the unanticipated degree of involvement of the club's female members, the inadequacy of the stables, the evolving interests of the members and an apparently increased need to generate revenue from the facility. Accordingly, the club was significantly remodeled and expanded between 1894 and 1905.[200]

In the summer and fall of 1894, the interior of the clubhouse was entirely reconfigured. Most significantly, the whole second floor was redesigned for the exclusive use of the club's female members (the men were consequently given the basement, though it was hardly a demotion—it was provided a large plunge bath, decorated in tile and fed by an artesian well). Another seating gallery was added to the riding hall, which increased its capacity from about eight hundred to over one thousand.

The club also required more space to store its members' horses, carriages and equipment. Accordingly, the club purchased the adjoining lot for $34,400, bringing its property line to Flatbush Avenue.[201] The directors had originally intended to build an expansion over the entire lot, but it was subsequently decided to divide the plot and build a smaller annex on the adjacent 80 feet, retaining the other 50 by 110 feet for a later addition. Frank Freeman (who had previously designed the Germania Club) was given the commission.

Freeman adhered to Stratton's basic design, conceiving a simple two-story brick building with a large central arch. The arch contained the main entranceway and was flanked on both sides by three smaller arched windows. On the second story were five narrow windows framed by pilasters at either side of the central arch. The extension was thus effectively tied to

The 1895 carriage house extension.

the original complex by its central arch, which evoked those of the riding hall and clubhouse façade, while the second floor windows recalled the two small pavilions at the top of the clubhouse.

The purpose of the second floor became the source of some controversy. Some members had wanted to build a bicycle hall with storage racks and an indoor riding ring, while others were opposed. Such a feature would require a trussed roof, which would increase its cost from $16,000 to $24,000. In the end, the club was able to raise sufficient capital through a sale of bonds to build the riding ring, and the members opposed to the "silent steed"—perhaps also seeking to avoid a permanent schism—backed down from the threat of legal action. The carriage house was completed in December 1895. After the carriages were relocated inside, one hundred additional stalls were added to the stable, bringing its total capacity to three hundred.

As bicycles had been all the rage in the mid-1890s, it was the automobile that challenged for supremacy in the early 1900s. By 1904, enough members owned cars to convince the club to make accommodation for their vehicles. Accordingly, a garage was constructed over the last remaining parcel of open space, the 110- by 50-foot plot adjacent to the 1895 extension, and completed in December 1905 at a cost of $35,000.[202] Though faced in brick, the entire structure—walls, floors, staircases and roof—was actually of heavy poured concrete. The garage contained three

The 1905 garage facing onto Plaza Street. *Courtesy of the New York Transit Museum.*

The Riding and Driving Club from Flatbush Avenue, 1917. The cut for the Grand Army Plaza IRT station exit is visible in the foreground to the left. *Courtesy of the New York Transit Museum.*

levels: a basement for the use of electric cars (with ten charging stations); a ground-level parking garage (with four entrances, three facing Flatbush and one onto Plaza Street); and a second floor with long-term parking, a chauffeur's lounge and a light machine shop. A large elevator connected the three floors, and a gashouse was located outside and to the rear. The garage could accommodate about one hundred cars, but it was anticipated that a third floor would eventually be added to complete the balance and symmetry of the entire complex. At the time, it was joked that this would be needed for flying machines that would supersede the automobile, as the automobile had eclipsed the horse and bicycle before it. As it were, the two-story garage was the final addition to the club, whose facilities now consisted of five distinct structures: the 1890 clubhouse, riding ring and stables; the 1895 carriage house; and the 1905 garage. From the corner of Flatbush, the finished complex appeared quite rambling as it curved around Plaza Street toward Vanderbilt Avenue.

Much of the club's early success had to do with the astute leadership of William Nelson Dykman, club president from 1893 to 1914.[203] Born on October 11, 1855, in Cold Spring, New York, Dykman graduated from the United States Military Academy in 1875. Assigned to the Twenty-second U.S. Infantry, he was involved in the pursuit of the Sioux chief Sitting Bull following Custer's defeat at Little Big Horn. Although he resigned his commission in 1877 to pursue a career in law, he continued to be affectionately called "Colonel Dykman" (although he never actually reached the rank). Admitted to the bar in 1878, he subsequently served as counsel to a number of corporations, eventually settling into the practice of Cullen and Dykman (which still maintains its original office at 177 Montague Street in Brooklyn Heights). Intelligent, highly respected and a skillful organizer, he was the perfect leader for the club's early years.

Like Dykman, many club members had prior experience in the cavalry. There was also a long-standing interest in military equestrianism at the club, which manifested itself in a number of ways. There were specialized riding classes, and beginning in the late 1890s—as the nation edged closer to war with Spain—military categories were added to the annual horseshow. These proved exceedingly popular and, by the Twentieth Annual Show (1912), were showcased over one entire evening. As the drums of war echoed across the Atlantic, a military endurance and control ride—the first contest outside the tanbark arena—was introduced in 1915. In support of the war effort, the club also dedicated all of the proceeds of the 1918 show, some $15,691.48, to the Red Cross.[204]

As far back as the 1890s, consideration had been given to formalizing the martial exercises of the members into some sort of officially sanctioned military or police unit. These failed to materialize, largely because there was no compelling need for their volunteer services. With the outbreak of the First World War, however, opportunity presented itself to directly contribute to the nation's war footing. In the spring of 1918, New York City police commissioner Richard Enright formed the New York Police Reserve to help buttress the ranks of the city police thinned by service in the war. Club member George H. Trumpler, a former cavalry officer who had been training members and select visitors (including students from Columbia University) on cavalry and military riding techniques, approached Enright about forming a unit at the club. The offer was enthusiastically received, and the Troop B Mounted Police Reserve, under the auspices and sponsorship of the club, was born.[205]

Though it was trained and prepared to conduct police operations, Troop B was largely utilized in symbolic roles. It was an escort at the graduation of the Navy Yard Electrical Class on April 12, 1918, and marched at the Red Cross Parade of May 18, 1918. The unit was deployed on several occasions for crowd control, notably at a postwar speech by the virulently anti-Kaiser James M. Beck at the Brooklyn Academy of Music in January 1919. It was a tense situation, with a large, boisterous crowd of veterans and rumors of a possible bomb plot swirling about. Though these ultimately proved unfounded, Troop B performed well under the circumstances. Following the war, the unit was demobilized, and Trumpler, who lived at 253 Garfield Place, went on to a distinguished career in the Kings County Grand Jurors Association as a forceful advocate for prison reform. The New York Police Reserve itself was not officially disbanded until April 9, 1934, when the shields, uniforms, nightsticks and firearms of its inactive volunteers were systematically collected.

The conclusion of the First World War and the dawn of the Roaring Twenties ushered another halcyon age for the club. Membership remained strong, as did public interest in the club's events, as demonstrated by the phenomenal success of the 1926 horseshow. There was also a move away from the earlier, more martial disposition of the club; the Great War had ended any romance of *Dulce et decorum est pro patria mori*.[206] Rather, in a decade of inherent tension and contradictions—the freewheeling laxity of jazz, the enforced morality of Prohibition—the club found the necessary balance, meeting the changing needs and interests of its members and the sporting public.

The Late, Great Brooklyn Riding and Driving Club

There were, however, the occasional missteps. On the evening of Tuesday, April 25, 1922, the Revered Dr. James E. Crowther, an esteemed Philadelphia pastor, was invited to give a talk at the club.[207] Crowther was famous for his production of *Wayfarer*, a three-hour religious extravaganza that had played for six weeks to sold-out audiences at New York's Madison Square Garden. A staunch supporter of Prohibition, the pastor had been assured that the club's members were churchgoers of upright probity. What the good pastor found at the Riding and Driving Club, however, he later described as a "feast of Belshazzar." Whiskey was poured openly, and his own glass was freely filled. Crowther departed before his speech, and later returned his twenty-five-dollar honorarium. Speaking on behalf of the club, member (and judge) Martin T. Manton carefully chose his words. He didn't deny that the reverend might have seen violations of the Volstead Act (which outlawed the sale or distribution of liquor) but maintained that the spirit of the Constitution was never violated. The legal nuance may have been rather spurious, but the status of its lector was not. The casual response betrays a confidence borne of the stature and standing of its members.

Throughout the club's history, in fact, much of its success had to do with the support, participation and advocacy of its influential members. This was important, as the club was quite difficult to manage and expensive to run. It required a large number of staff, daily operation and frequent maintenance. Over time, its leadership developed increasingly diverse revenue sources, which eventually included initiation fees, annual dues, instructional fees, rentals, sponsored events and the leasing of the riding hall to outside parties. In addition, variably priced tickets were sold to some events (such as the horseshow). This is interesting, as it generally (if loosely) corresponds to the diverse revenue model of more traditional sports facilities. This dynamism was due, in part, to a series of committed and effective leaders. As Smith had once led the efforts to establish the club, and Dykman its glory years of the 1890s and 1900s, the multi-year presidency of Thomas Leeming defined and nurtured the success of the early 1920s.

Thomas Lonsdale Leeming was born in Montreal on January 9, 1872. An 1894 graduate of the Columbia University School of Mines, he went on to a successful career in business, where, in addition to the management of his own pharmaceutical importing firm of Thomas Leeming & Co., he was vice-president of Nestlé's Food Company and director of the Dime Savings Bank. He lived with his wife and three children in a mansion at

94 Eighth Avenue (previously owned by Timothy Woodruff). In addition to being a long-serving president of the Riding and Driving Club, he was also director of the Brooklyn Academy of Music and a trustee of Adelphi College. He was deeply committed to the cultural, social and intellectual life of Brooklyn and universally admired and respected.

He also harbored a secret. On the morning of June 5, 1925, he was accosted by a drug-addicted drifter named Charles Muller in the crowded lobby of his Manhattan office at 130 William Street. A shouting match ensued, and Leeming asked that Muller be removed from the premises. As Leeming turned to enter the elevator, Muller shot him with a .25-caliber pistol hidden in the pocket of his coat. He fled the scene but was apprehended several blocks away. Leeming was rushed to Beekman Street Hospital but died shortly afterward.[208]

As the police later reconstructed, the two had met some years before in the Catskill Mountains. They had remained in contact, but in December 1924 Muller began blackmailing Leeming. Leeming had confided of this to John McQuade, treasurer of Thomas Leeming & Co, but steadfastly refused to report it to the police on account of the scandal that it would cause. A subsequent search of Muller's personal effects uncovered another pistol, ten pawn tickets, a massage machine, letters of financial support from Leeming and—in the nuanced language of one of the detectives—pictures of "a certain kind."[209]

Leeming was memorialized in a service at Central Congregation Church on Hancock Street on the afternoon of Monday, June 8.[210] More than five hundred mourners came to pay their respects, including delegations from the Brooklyn Academy of Music and the Riding and Driving Club (led by the seventy-year-old Colonel Dykman). In response to the shockingly brazen murder, Mayor John Hylan convened a committee to look into the problem of gun ownership and possession in the city, setting the foundation for New York City's tough gun control laws.[211] At the Riding and Driving Club, Leeming's family established a $1,500 trophy in his name for the annual horseshow, first awarded at the gala thirty-fourth annual show in 1926.[212]

The beginning of 1926 proved trying as well. That January, an epidemic of spinal meningitis swept the stables, sickening a number of horses.[213] After two died, the stables were quarantined for a week. Dr. Charles J. Pflug, a well-connected member, obtained permission from the police to close off Plaza Street so that the horses could be exercised in the fresh air. Though not the first epidemic to strike the stable, it was by far the most traumatic and deadly.

While the members were grateful for Dr. Pflug's intercession, it was another Pflug who was the perpetual toast of the club for the latter part of the 1920s: Dr. Pflug's son Carl was the leading player on the club's championship indoor polo team, which is widely considered to be one of the best ever.

Polo had a long history at the club.[214] It had fielded an outdoor team from 1896 to '98 and again from 1906 to '20 under the auspices of the Polo Association. That team, whose colors—personally selected by Colonel Dykman—were white with lilac dots, had played their home games in the meadows of Prospect Park. Starting in 1910, the club also sponsored an indoor polo team in the short-lived National Indoor Polo Association. In 1915, the Indoor Polo Association (IPA) was formed, and by 1921, the Brooklyn Riding and Driving Club had become one of its fifteen teams, playing under its old Polo Association colors.

The best ever? Championship indoor polo team of the Brooklyn Riding and Driving Club, circa 1929. *Courtesy of Photography Collection, Miriam and Ira D. Wallach Division of Arts, Prints and Photographs, New York Public Library.*

The IPA standardized the rules and regulations of the sport, including the use of a soft (and consequently safer) ball. Though games were played at larger facilities (such as regional armories), the sport struggled with the variations in field size and surface quality, which had a tendency to provide advantage to the "home" team. Nonetheless, in a world where equestrian sports were popular, the sport gained an avid following. In 1921, four championship classes were established: the senior, junior, rookie and intercollegiate. In each category, the winning team was awarded a trophy; that in the junior category was donated by Thomas Leeming. In subsequent years, the categories were reorganized, and the senior became Class A, the junior Class C and the rookie Class D. The Intercollegiate Trophy was eliminated, and a new secondary ranking, Class B, was added. Finally, in 1926, a new class was introduced: the Open Championship, which became the premier prize in the sport.

In 1927, the Riding and Driving Club fielded a team that consisted of Carl Pflug, Gerard Smith and Warren Sackman. As required, all three were club members; Sackman also happened to be Jewish, which heretofore had been rather exceptional. That year, the team swept away the competition, taking the Open Championship, as well as the Class A and Class C Championships. In 1928 and 1929, it again captured the Open Championship. In 1930, the team made it to the Open finals, where it lost to the Optimists, who were led by the sport's first ten-goal player, Winston Guest. Nonetheless, it was a dominant and unmatched three-year run. In 1931, a subsequent team took home the Class B Championship, which was the last ever won by the club.

MEMBER-RESIDENTS OF SPORTSMEN'S ROW

As with the Montauk Club, membership in the Brooklyn Riding and Driving Club represented the paragon of social prestige and distinction.[215] At the same time, the club's specificity of purpose permitted it to draw members from all over Brooklyn but also restricted it to those with interest in equestrianism. Consequently, it had fewer members along northern Eighth Avenue than its sister club. Not surprisingly, neither Garrison nor Rowe nor the Dwyers were members; even if there had been interest, social standing would have been an issue. Ironically, Garrison might have

Number 117 Sterling Place, originally a stable. Snapper Garrison lodged his horse and buggy here.

actually made for a good fit. He was known to greatly enjoy riding for recreation and pleasure.[216]

Local tradition has maintained that the sportsmen did at least stable their domestic horses and carriages at the club. This is a logical inference, given the club's proximity and the fact that it did lease space to nonmembers. Though our sources are meager in this regard, there is no evidence of any such association. Furthermore, a curious incident in Garrison's life on Sportsmen's Row confirms otherwise, at least insomuch as he is concerned.[217] On the night of November 13, 1893, Garrison's personal driver, John McGinley, absconded with the jockey's prized horse and buggy after dropping him off at number 30. Garrison was notified of the theft by the private stable at 117 Sterling Place, where he lodged his $1,200 horse and brougham carriage. Garrison tracked down McGinley the next morning, finding him, after a night of joy riding, at the intersection of Bowery and Grand Street in New York City. Beyond their mutual engagement in equestrian sports, it seems that the club's connection with the sportsmen of Sportsmen's Row was, in fact, entirely coincidental.

Of the other residents of Sportsmen's Row, Gaynor, Goepel and Hyde were at one time or another members, as was Robert Pinkerton. Valentine Schmitt, always something of an outsider on the block, was another committed horseman, but his loyalties lay with the Arion Riding Club.[218] Though the Riding and Driving Club provided one bookend to Sportsmen's Row, the divide of Flatbush Avenue was seemingly quite distant. In fact, until the building of Spite Row, the block's relationship was not much more than a convenient shortcut for those hurrying to the club.

The qualities that made the Brooklyn Riding and Driving Club so special—its singularity, exclusivity and prime location—also made it exceedingly vulnerable to the seismic shifts that would soon sweep Brooklyn. It had been born of the same milieu as the Montauk Club, with which it evolved in lockstep. Their respective fates, however, would be quite different.

GARRISON FINISH

As Gaynor's funeral procession receded into memory, Brooklyn faced a difficult road ahead. Although consolidation had benefitted the greater metropolitan area, the now borough of Brooklyn would be rent asunder by the cataclysmic changes that transpired in its wake. The reasons were many—the expansion of mass transit, the increasing "pull" of Manhattan and the suburbs and, later, postwar deindustrialization—but the end was the same. Several decades into the twentieth century, Brooklyn was noticeably poorer. By the 1950s, much of Park Slope had in fact become little more than an urban slum—"in transition" was one contemporary euphemism[219]—filled with increasing numbers of ramshackle rooming houses, abandoned properties and empty storefronts. Banks began redlining the area, while unscrupulous "blockbusters" coerced many of the remaining homeowners to sell their properties at fire sale prices, suggesting that they get out before things got even worse. By 1960, the neighborhood was in deplorable condition.

The change had begun slowly, around the turn of the century, when apartment buildings began to predominate among new construction. Though many of these were quite elegant, their intended market was quite clear: a more middle-class resident, for whom the mansion and town house were too large and expensive. At the same time, many of Brooklyn's more affluent residents began departing for Manhattan or the suburbs. By the 1920s, they were doing so en masse. The housing stock that they left behind—the opulent town houses and aureate mansions—were largely

Old Sportsmen's Row from Flatbush Avenue, 1962. The building on the corner is extant, though now shorn of its detailing. *Courtesy of the New York Transit Museum.*

unaffordable or inappropriate to the borough's newest inhabitants; they were also often seen as obsolescent and undesirable. Accordingly, most of the grand residences were demolished—that of J. Rogers Maxwell went in 1922, Tilyou's around 1929, Hanan's about 1935 and Feltman's in 1950—while many of the town houses were reconfigured, their stoops removed and interiors carved up into multiple units. Even as the legacy of Brooklyn's glorious past was being rapidly and unceremoniously extirpated all around, some hailed these efforts as a necessary step toward modernity.[220]

Sportsmen's Row was not immune to these changes. With the opening of the Grand Army Plaza subway stop on August 23, 1920, the area experienced increased pedestrian traffic: one of its exits was located adjacent to the small apartment building (once owned by Hyde and Behman) at the corner of Flatbush Avenue and another directly opposite the Riding and Driving Club. In 1927, the Hyde and Behman apartment building was sold

152

to developers, and in its place was erected a sixteen-story apartment building, completed in the following year (1 Plaza Street).[221] Though it towers over the neighboring brownstones, its orientation toward Flatbush Avenue does somewhat exclude it from the fabric of the block; it feels as alien as the neighboring houses of Spite Row.

In the late summer of 1945, Gaynor's old residence at number 20 was sold to the Berk and Coughlin Construction Company. The firm subsequently "modernized" the house, stripping its interior of much of its ornate plasterwork and wood detailing and dividing it up into eight smaller units. The company also removed the stoop and the elegant mayor's lamps with which the house had been graced since Gaynor's mayoralty. On the occasion, the *Brooklyn Daily Eagle* provided a brief—and notably inaccurate—history of Sportsmen's Row:[222]

> *The block in which the Gaynor home is located was long known as "Sportsmen's Row" because of the residents identified with horseracing at the time. Among them were the Dwyer brothers, part owners of the Coney Island Jockey Club racetrack, Jimmy McLoughlin [sic], famous jockey of the time, and Henry W. Behman and John H. Hyde, owners of Hyde and Behmans' vaudeville theater. Others living on the block were Mirabeau Towns, known as the "poet lawyer," Mayor Alfred C. Chapin, [and] Judge James Troy...*

It would be the last printed reference to Sportsmen's Row.

The neighborhood was changing in other ways as well. The proliferation of cars had steadily replaced the horse as the primary means of local transportation; even the Riding and Driving Club had been forced to address this in 1905. Local streets grew ever more congested as trolleys, trucks, cars and the remaining horses and wagons jockeyed for position. Eighth Avenue became particularly treacherous, with vehicles barreling down its broad straightaway. In December 1919, an overloaded city bus speeding along at thirty miles per hour collided with a trolley as it turned from Eighth onto Flatbush Avenue.[223] The bus overturned and was almost completely destroyed. Though there were no fatalities, some twenty-five injured passengers were carried into the garage of the Riding and Driving Club, where they were triaged before being taken to the hospital. Soon thereafter, a group of concerned Eighth Avenue residents petitioned the public service commissioner to end bus service along the avenue. Among its signatories were Towns, Troy, Shevlin and Anna

Pinkerton, in something of a final show of civic unity for what remained of old Sportsmen's Row.

As the neighborhood changed around it, the Riding and Driving Club struggled to stay afloat. Already expensive to run, it was now losing members in droves and was increasingly situated amid tall buildings and traffic-choked streets. In 1926, it initiated formal discussion with the Montauk Club about merging. The plan was to sell both clubhouses and build another, under the auspices of the Montauk Riding and Driving Club of Brooklyn.[224] Two years later, a new plan was suggested, which called for the demolition of the Riding and Driving Club and the erection of a new fifteen-story clubhouse designed by H. Craig Severance (best known for his 1930 skyscraper at 40 Wall Street). This was to contain a clubhouse, riding ring, gymnasium, swimming pool and courts for tennis and squash. In the end, neither this nor any merger came to fruition.

In 1936, amid declining attendance, the annual horseshow was moved to Teevan's Riding Academy, which was located diagonally across Prospect Park in an area that was less congested and home to several small riding establishments. In 1938, the club formally disbanded, though its facility was briefly used as a riding school and a meeting place for several local churches. In the latter part of the year, the riding ring served as a public garage. Early the next year, the largely abandoned complex was purchased for $250,000. The clubhouse and riding hall were subsequently demolished, and a six-story apartment building was erected in its place (20 Plaza Street).[225] The club's original carriage house and garage were used as a commercial garage until 1959, when they too were torn down and replaced by a fifteen-story apartment building (10 Plaza Street). Teevan's, the putative successor to the Brooklyn Riding and Driving Club, managed to hang on until 1955, when it was converted into a bowling alley. All of its neighboring riding establishments closed soon thereafter, save one. Now known as the Kensington Stable, it is one of Brooklyn's last equestrian institutions, home to forty-one horses, one carriage and a faded copy of the 1919 Brooklyn Horse Show catalogue.

As horses increasingly disappeared from public life, the public's interest in spectator sports—perhaps not coincidentally—also began to change. Baseball became increasingly popular, ultimately supplanting horse racing as the preeminent spectator sport. Though horse racing did retain its fans, its ongoing image problem—the associated gambling and crime, in particular—brought it continued scrutiny and censure. In 1910, Governor Charles Evans Hughes banned the sport, effectively closing all of the

The 1895 and 1905 club extensions in use as a public garage, 1939. Note the building behind (20 Plaza Street) where the riding hall was previously located. *Courtesy of New York City Municipal Archives.*

The successors of the Brooklyn Riding and Driving Club. Clockwise from the left: Kensington Stable, an unidentified stable and the site of Teevan's Riding Club.

state's tracks; in the 1909 mayoral race, one of William Ivins's accusations against Gaynor was that the judge was conspiring with racing interests to thwart the impending legislation. Although the ban was lifted in 1913, Brooklyn's three great racetracks never reopened, and the sport shifted to Long Island's Jamaica, Aqueduct and Belmont tracks.[226] The Brooklyn Jockey Club formally folded in 1916, and its major stakes, including the Brooklyn Handicap, were transferred to Aqueduct. The Gravesend racetrack itself saw limited use for other entertainments, including baseball and music concerts, but was eventually sold to developers. The racetrack was demolished in the 1920s to provide land for middle-class housing; as one of the last directors of the club, it was Shevlin who ultimately saw to its dénouement.[227]

Back on Eighth Avenue, the Montauk Club managed to hang on through the lean years. Some of this was due to the quality of its leadership—club presidents Frank Russell (served 1931–48) and Edward T. Carvin (1948–60) are particularly noteworthy in this regard—as well as a seeming knack for adaptation. At Depew's seventy-fifth birthday address (1909), Depew's wife and Mrs. Calvin Coolidge attended the reception and dined with the men in the main dining room. It was a first. Though women had been welcomed in the club from its inception and had their own quarters, it was largely a male domain. Subsequently, the sexes mingled with greater frequency, and women were permitted use of the bowling alley. In the same year, Rabbi Alexander Lyons of Temple Beth Elohim (located at the corner of Eighth Avenue and Garfield Street) was extended an honorary membership. As the neighborhood (and the times) changed, the club managed to become more inclusive, while simultaneously remaining sufficiently (or at least economically) exclusive. Among the notable speakers it drew in this era were Herbert Hoover, Dwight Eisenhower, John F. Kennedy (bringing its presidential total to seven) and Senator Robert F. Kennedy. Ironically, one of its most popular events of the 1960s was a day at the races—primarily at Aqueduct. Though many decades after the fact, it brought the club and the sportsmen, at long last, into alignment.

The Montauk Club's survival was also due, in part, to the fact that northern Eighth Avenue and Plaza Street had fared better than many of the other surrounding blocks. As such, the immediate vicinity provided it just enough members to remain in operation. Although Eighth Avenue held its share of rooming houses—the so-called Ardwell at numbers 46 and 50 was particularly notorious—the stretch had become something of a "Doctor's Row" and was home to a good number of medical offices (a circumstance that remains to the present day). Notably, one of the club's most prominent members in the 1950s and '60s was Dr. Harold R. Merwarth, a well-regarded neuro-psychiatrist who lived in Snapper Garrison's old house at number 30 (and the honoree of a club dinner on November 14, 1963).

Along what was once Sportsmen's Row, all of the houses, save numbers 14, 16 and 22, had been converted into multi-family residences by the 1950s. Although the block remained livable enough, the general grittiness and decay of much of the surrounding area—especially along and across Flatbush Avenue and to the west starting around Sixth Avenue—brought a general sense of insecurity and disorder. One July evening in 1951, a man seeking relief from the heat managed to find his way onto the roof of number 10, where he fell asleep; he was likely intoxicated. Sometime in the early morning, he rolled off onto the projecting bay window below and died.[228] To the residents of numbers 8–10—now an eighteen-unit apartment building with three ground-floor doctor's offices—it would have been a most unsettling incident.

Park Slope plane crash, corner of Seventh Avenue and Sterling Place, December 16, 1960. *Courtesy of the Brooklyn Public Library, Brooklyn Collection.*

Park Slope's nadir came on the morning of December 16, 1960, when United Airlines Flight 826 crashed into the intersection of Seventh Avenue and Sterling Place after colliding with a smaller plane over the harbor. All 128 passengers on board the planes perished, as did 6 people on the ground (one initial survivor, eleven-year-old Stephen Baltz, subsequently died at Methodist Hospital). Wreckage was strewn all over the neighborhood, and a number of buildings were destroyed, including the ironically named Pillar of Fire Church. The subheadline that appeared the next day in the *New York Times* read, "Sterling Place, an Area of Run-Down Houses." It was only two blocks from the stretch once known as Sportsmen's Row.

And then, in the mid-1960s, something remarkable began to happen. The pendulum began to swing back. Park Slope was "rediscovered" by a new generation of young professionals who began moving to the neighborhood. Despite the depredations and general neglect, the area was still well located and attractive and continued to retain some sense of charm and intimacy—characteristics that many felt to be absent in the depersonalized nature of suburban sprawl and urban overbuild. And, not to mention, it was also now quite affordable. Within a few years, a vibrant sense of community was (re-) established as long-neglected brownstones were renovated, shops (re-) opened along the commercial byways and such neighborhood institutions as the Park Slope Food Coop were established. In a remarkable display of corporate and private cooperation, the efforts of these so-called brownstoners were aided by the Brooklyn Union Gas Company, which established the Cinderella Project in 1966 to renovate derelict brownstones and encourage homeownership. The company had the foresight to recognize that a vibrant community would benefit its bottom line. These remarkable efforts would culminate in the granting of landmark status to most of north Park Slope, including old Sportsmen's Row, in July 1973. Director Hal Ashby masterfully portrayed this tumultuous era, with its tension between urban decay and gentrification, in his 1970 film set in Park Slope, *The Landlord*.

The names of the brownstoners are the stuff of local legend: Evelyn and Everett Ortner, Bob Makla, Joe Ferris, William Younger and Clem Labine (who founded the *Old House Journal* to promote the idea of renovation), to name just a few. Old Sportsmen's Row would also play a role in this revitalization. In 1963, John Cassara and his partner, Charlie Brown, purchased number 22 Eighth Avenue (they would later also buy numbers 20 and 26). In 1973, after having difficulty collecting an insurance claim on number 22, Cassara established the Brownstone Agency, an insurance firm that offered policies specifically for brownstone owners.[229] The company provided, among other considerations, explicit coverage for many of the unique architectural features of the brownstone. Almost instantly, Cassara filled a pressing need for local reclamation efforts. Brown, meanwhile, worked in real estate, where he had been trying to sell a vacant restaurant at 342–52 Flatbush Avenue, right around the corner from Sportsmen's Row.[230] The space had once housed a local institution known as Michel's, which had opened in 1910 and closed on January 1, 1975. In its early years, the restaurant had advertised in the Riding and Driving Club's annual horseshow catalogue and was later frequented by many of the Brooklyn Dodgers. Brown had difficulty finding a buyer, so in 1978 he purchased the place himself and opened his own establishment, Charlie's. In the spirit of Val Schmitt before him, Brown's restaurant soon became a local favorite—and prefigured the culinary destination that Park Slope would soon become.

Michel's restaurant, 342–52 Flatbush Avenue.

Although number 22 was in fairly good condition, Cassara and Brown added a pair of magnificent sconces to its exterior. These were *spoilia* from Manhattan's Plaza-Savoy Hotel (demolished in 1964), and their large size and ornamentation have caused them to be misidentified as the mayoral lamps that once flanked number 20. This is why number 22 is so frequently believed to be Gaynor's house. In 1987, Cassara and Brown sold number 22 and 342–52 Flatbush Avenue, which sadly had its original interior gutted by the subsequent tenant, Blockbuster Video.

By the end of the twentieth century, Park Slope had returned to the affluent and desirable neighborhood it had been just a century before. Brownstones, which only forty years ago could be had for next to nothing, now regularly sell for millions. Brown and Cassara, for instance, had purchased number 22 for $43,000 (about $306,000 in 2010, and admittedly expensive at the time) and eventually cooped and sold the three units for a little under $2,000,000; in 2012, the simplex apartment on the second floor alone sold for $1,189,000. Though gentrification has certainly brought its share of problems and challenges, it is worth recalling that Park Slope's mid-century malaise was, in fact, more the exception in its history.

The Montauk Club remains a private social club to this day, the last of what were once many in Brooklyn.[231] Though the bowling alley is now leased

Number 22 Eighth Avenue. Its large, ornate sconces have been the source of much confusion.

as office space and its upper floors became condominiums in 1996, the club presently engages a new and markedly younger clientele who have brought with them a newfound sense of energy and purpose. Both the club and its associated block—old Sportsmen's Row—are now frequently used for film and television productions. Considering how far and fast the neighborhood had fallen in the postwar years, it is truly a remarkable turn of affairs—and, appropriately, very much a Garrison Finish.

NOTES

In the interest of conserving space, endnotes have been provided in an abbreviated format.

BDE = *Brooklyn Daily Eagle*
CDT = *Chicago Daily Tribune*
NYT = *New York Times*
NYTR = *New York Tribune*
PSHDDR = *Park Slope Historic District Designation Report*
RERBG = *Real Estate Record and Builder's Guide*
TR = *Thoroughbred Record*
WaPo = *Washington Post*

INTRODUCTION

1. O'Hanlon, "Neighborhood Change," 133ff; Cudahy, *How We Got to Coney Island*, chs. 2, 4.

2. The 1890 census apparently indicated that the neighborhood had the highest per capita income of any in the nation. Though a good portion of the census was destroyed by fire in 1921, this fact seems to be popularly accepted; Trager, *New York Chronology*, 224.

CHAPTER 1

3. As northern Park Slope was then more commonly called.

4. *NYTR*, April 20, 1884, 4.

5. *PSHDDR*, 15.

6. About U.S. $570,000 in 2010.

7. *CDT*, October 7, 1888, 15; *BDE*, February 5, 1889, 6; February 13, 1889, 6; Robertson, *History of Thoroughbred Racing*, 166.

8. *BDE*, April 19, 1893, 1; *NYT*, August 20, 1906, 7.

9z. *NYTR*, August 20, 1906, 2; *CDT*, October 7, 1888, 15.

10. *NYT*, June 24, 1900, 18.

11. *NYTR*, August 19, 1890, 7; *BDE*, April 19, 1893, 1.

12. *WaPo*, September 11, 1887, 1; *CDT*, May 6, 1888, 13; May 29, 1888, 6; May 31, 1888, 3; August 30, 1888, 3; October 7, 1888, 15; *BDE*, May 29, 1888, 6; May 31, 1888, 6; *NYT*, August 29, 1888, 2; *NYTR*, September 2, 1888, 3.

13. *CDT*, May 31, 1888, 3.

14. Ibid., October 7, 1888, 15.

15. *BDE*, May 31, 1888, 6.

16. Quoted in *CDT*, August 30, 1888, 3.

17. *NYT*, November 15, 1913, 3.

18. *PSHDDR*, 13.

19. *BDE*, February 13, 1889, 6.

20. Ibid., January 16, 1889, 5; January 23, 1889, 4; February 5, 1889, 6; February 6, 1889, 4, 6; February 7, 1889, 6; February 13, 1889, 6.

21. Ibid., February 5, 1889, 6.

22. Ibid., February 6, 1889, 6.

23. Ibid., May 17, 1889, 1.

24. Ibid., January 23, 1889, 4.

25. Ibid., February 13, 1889, 6.

26. Ibid.

27. Ibid., October 21, 1892, 2.

28. Ibid., June 21, 1889, 6.

29. Robertson, *History of Thoroughbred Racing*, 167; *NYT*, January 14, 1889, 2; October 29, 1930, 18; *WaPo*, May 10, 1908, M3; *Blood Horse*, November 8, 1930, 1323; *TR*, November 1, 1930, 293.

30. *NYT*, October 29, 1930, 18.

31. *PSHDDR*, 16.

32. Ibid., 13.

33. *BDE*, April 11, 1891,1.

34. *PSHDDR*, 15.

35. Bowen, "James Rowe Sr."; *BDE*, September 16, 1900, 10; *TR* 1, no. 10 (1929), 88.

36. Black, *King of Fifth Avenue*, 718.

37. *NYT*, August 19, 1890, 3; *NYTR*, August 18, 1890, 12; August 19, 1890, 7.

38. *NYTR*, August 18, 1890, 12.

39. Ibid., August 19, 1890, 7.

40. *BDE*, June 3, 1891, 1; *NYT*, June 3, 1891, 5.

41. *BDE*, June 4, 1891, 5.

42. *BDE*, December 15, 1892, 12; *RERBG* 48, no. 1226 (September 12, 1891), 331; *PSHDDR*, 15.

43. *American Architect and Building News* 105, no. 1 (February 25, 1914), 5.

Chapter 2

44. *BDE*, June 21, 1892, 6.

45. In 1892, $1.00 = about $24.70 in 2010.

46. *BDE*, March 31, 1893, 1; *NYTR*, March 26, 1893, 21; April 2, 1893, 21.

47. Cited in *BDE*, March 31, 1893, 1.

48. Lancaster, *Gentlemen of the Press*, 161.

49. *BDE*, April 19, 1893, 1; *NYTR*, April 20, 1893, 10.

50. *BDE*, June 29, 1893, 10.

51. *Boston Globe*, December 17, 1893, 6; *NYT*, December 17, 1893, 2.

52. *BDE*, December 22, 1893, 5; December 23, 1893, 10; *NYT*, December 24, 1893, 2.

53. *BDE*, January 1, 1890, 6; January 4, 1890, 6; January 19, 1890, 14; April 7, 1890, 6; *NYTR*, January 2, 1890, 10; *CDT*, July 6, 1891, 6.

54. *NYTR*, January 2, 1890, 10.

55. Ibid.

56. Ibid.

57. *NYT*, June 26, 1891, 2; *Boston Globe*, June 29, 1891, 9.

58. *BDE*, August 25, 1896, 3.

59. Ibid., December 7, 1896, 4); *The Sun*, December 9, 1896, 6.

60. Though it was the Merriam-Webster word of the day for November 17, 2006: http://www.merriam-webster.com/cgi-bin/mwwodarch.pl?November.17.2006.

61. Bowen, "James Rowe Sr.," 22; *TR* 42 (1895), 34.

62. *TR* 42 (1895), 34.

63. Bowen (2007), 9-10.

64. *Weekly Irish Times*, February 1, 1890, 2.

65. *NYT*, August 20, 1906, 7; *NYTR*, August 20, 1906, 1.

66. *NYT*, August 22, 1909, 9; June 10, 1917, 6; June 15, 1917, 9; *WaPo*, June 10, 1917, 2; June 13, 1917, 12.

67. *BDE*, July 24, 1949, 21.

68. Ibid., November 26, 1895, 1.

CHAPTER 3

69. Ierardi, *Gravesend*, 98ff; Vosburgh, *Racing in America*, 30–31; Kapsales, "From the Gilded Age," 15ff; *BDE*, March 4,1886, 4; *NYT*, July 19, 1886, 8; August 24, 1886, 2; *NYTR*, August 2, 1886, 8.

70. *BDE*, August 26, 1886, 4; August 27, 1886, 2; *NYT*, August 27, 1886, 3; *NYTR*, August 27, 1886, 8.

71. Morn, *Eye That Never Sleeps*, 112–13.

72. Jarman, "Great Racetrack Caper"; Riess, *Sport of Kings*, 197ff.

73. Schwartz, *Roll the Bones*, 333ff; Riess, *Sport of Kings*, 34ff, 79ff.

74. *PSHDDR*, 16. Horan and Swiggett, *Pinkerton Story*, 250–51; number 71 is incorrectly noted.

75. *BDE*, February 29, 1892, 2.

76. *PSHDDR*, 17.

77. *BDE*, November 14, 1900, 13; November 15, 1900, 10; *NYT*, November 15, 1900, 7.

78. *NYT*, April 11, 1904, 1; April 12, 1904, 2; April 21, 1904, 16; *NYTR*, April 11, 1904, 1.

79. http://money.cnn.com/2010/09/16/news/companies/grocery_coop_Brooklyn.fortune/index.htm.

80. *NYT*, August 18, 1907, 7; *WaPo*, September 21, 1907, 2.

81. *NYT*, November 4, 1930, 13.

82. Ibid., November 22, 1933, 19.

83. *BDE*, March 3, 1886, 4.

84. Rogers, *Papers*, 254–55, no. 1; Howard, *Eagle and Brooklyn*, 994–95; *BDE*, December 16, 1912, 4.

85. *BDE*, December 13, 1888, 2.

86. Ibid., December 15, 1888, 1.

87. Ibid., January 27, 1893, 1.

88. Stewart, *No Applause*, 124–27; Cullen, *Vaudeville Old & New*, 1215–6; *NYT*, July 22, 1923, 5; Kartalis, "Percy William's Legacy," 3,10.

89. *BDE*, July 25, 1889, 6; August 2, 1889, 4.

90. Ibid., October 25, 1891, 2.

91. http://www.savestpauls.org/history.

92. *BDE*, May 4, 1894, 1.

93. Ibid., June 11, 1894, 2.

94. Ibid., May 24, 1894, 12; May 29, 1894, 7.

95. *In re Dwyer*, 14 Misc. 204, 70 N.Y.St.Rep. 546, 35 N.Y.S. 884 (1894); *BDE*, May 29, 1894, 7; Pink, *Gaynor*, 96; Thomas, *Mayor Who Mastered New York*, 89; Liebman, "Horseracing in New York," 550–62.

96. McCullough, *Good Old Coney Island*, 132; Pink, *Gaynor*, 95; *NYTR*, October 24, 1909, 1.

97. *NYT*, June 11, 1894, 9.

98. *BDE*, May 20, 1888, 6.

99. *NYT*, December 19, 1892, 2.

100. *NYT*, November 25, 1924, 23; Howard, *Eagle and Brooklyn*, 448.

101. *BDE*, February 13, 1896, 1.

102. *NYT*, October 3, 1936, 17.

103. *BDE*, March 25, 1894, 24.

104. Howard, *Eagle and Brooklyn*, 494–95; *Harper's Weekly*, July 29, 1911, 31; *NYT*, November 26, 1932, 10.

105. *Harper's Weekly*, July 29, 1911, 31.

106. *Eagle Savings and Loan Co. v. Samuels*, 43 A.D. 386 (N.Y. App. Div. 2d Dept. 1899); *NYT*, July 8, 1899, 12.

107. Ditta, *Gravesend*, 42.

108. Thomas, *Mayor Who Mastered New York*, 100, 106, 329–30; Pink, *Gaynor*, 197, 211–12.

109. *BDE*, May 16, 1894, 9.

110. Ibid., May 26, 1889, 16; June 16, 1889, 1.

111. Ibid., January 20, 1888, 3.

112. Ibid., July 25, 1883, 4; May 14, 1885, 2; September 25, 1886, 6.

113. McCullough, *Good Old Coney Island*, 38ff, 127; *NYT*, January 12, 1884, 5.

CHAPTER 4

114. *BDE*, January 21, 1897, 12; February 19, 1897, 12. He moved from 206 St. John's Place.

115. *BDE*, April 21, 1890, 6.

116. Ibid., June 20, 1896, 1; June 28, 1896, 17; July 8, 1896, 16; December 21, 1896, 3; *NYTR*, June 23, 1896, 13; June 28, 1896, 15.

117. *NYT*, July 7, 1900, 5; *BDE*, February 7, 1901, 1; February 8, 1901, 2; September 21, 1901, 15.

118. *BDE*, February 7, 1901, 1.

119. Ibid.

120. Ibid.

121. *PSHDDR*, 80.

122. *BDE*, September 21, 1901, 15.

123. Ibid., October 12, 1901, 17.

124. Ibid., July 9, 1900, 14; September 5, 1900, 2.

125. Ibid., October 28, 1901, 1; *NYTR*, October 28, 1901, 9.

126. Ibid., March 6, 1902, 1; *NYT*, February 23, 1902, 7; March 6, 1902, 9.

127. Ibid., October 11, 1898, 3; December 27, 1898, 3.

128. *NYT*, July 7, 1900, 6.

129. *BDE*, June 4, 1902, 2.

130. Number 220 Prospect Place for Mrs. Mary McMullen and 251 Prospect Place for Mrs. Nora Milde.

131. *NYT*, December 26, 1912, 1.

132. Ibid., March 18, 1913, 1; *BDE*, April 20, 1913, 3; February 8, 1915, 4.

133. *NYT*, December 18, 1914, 13.

134. *BDE*, October 9, 1901, 17.

135. *Ennis v. Federal Brewing Co.*, 108 N.Y.S. 230 (N.Y. App. Div. 2d Dept. 1908).

136. *BDE*, January 21, 1905, 13; August 12, 1907, 7.

137. Ibid., October 20, 1905, 6.

138. *NYT*, April 16, 1915, 13; *BDE*, March 6, 1917, 2.

139. *BDE*, April 13, 1928, 1.

140. *NYT*, August 14, 1930, 38.

141. *BDE*, August 6, 1939, B7.

142. Ibid., June 6, 1900, 22; *NYT*, June 7, 1900, 7.

143. *BDE*, September 1, 1904, 2.

144. *Memorial Cyclopedia*, 239–40.

145. *Das Deutsche Element*, 115.

146. Howard, *Eagle and Brooklyn*, 860–62.

147. *BDE*, January 11, 1901, 5.

148. *NYT*, March 6, 1940, 20.

149. *BDE*, December 28, 1912, 1; June 25, 1913, 7; *NYT*, June 25, 1913, 9.

150. *NY Dramatic Mirror*, January 8, 1913, 12.

151. *BDE*, December 27, 1917, 8.

CHAPTER 5

152. Pink, *Gaynor*; Smith, *William Jay Gaynor*; Thomas, *Mayor Who Mastered New York*; Gaynor, *Letters*.

153. Smith, *William Jay Gaynor*, 10

154 Pink, *Gaynor*, 63; Thomas, *Mayor Who Mastered New York*, 48.

155. Smith, *William Jay Gaynor*, 39.

156. Ibid., 41; Thomas, *Mayor Who Mastered New York*, 104–08, 125–26.

157. Incorrectly identified in Thomas, *Mayor Who Mastered New York*, 107, as rector of St. John's Protestant Episcopal Church. He was actually rector of All Saints Episcopal Church; *NYT*, April 9, 1896, 8. He lived at 143 Lincoln Place.

158. Pink, *Gaynor*, 129; Smith, *William Jay Gaynor*, 59; Thomas, *Mayor Who Mastered New York*, 156.

159. *NYT*, October 10, 1909, 2.

160. Ibid., October 14, 1909, 2; *NYTR*, October 12, 1909, 1; October 14, 1909, 1; Smith, *William Jay Gaynor*, 68–69.

161. Thomas, *Mayor Who Mastered New York*, 191.

162. Pink, *Gaynor*, 143.

163. *BDE*, June 10, 1910, 2.

CHAPTER 6

164. *Brooklyn Life*, "Montauk Club," 125; *Montauk Club*; *NYT*, December 15, 1889, 16; Howard, *Eagle and Brooklyn*, 918–19.

165. *BDE*, March 7, 1889, 1, 4; March 11, 1889, 2.

166. Ibid., March 20, 1889, 6.

167. Ibid., December 14, 1889, 6; *NYT*, December 15, 1889, 16.

168. Morrone, *Architectural Guidebook*, 341–44; *PSHDDR*, 13–14. There is no comprehensive study of the building's architecture.

169. *Brooklyn Life*, September 20, 1890, 12.

170. About U.S. $5,560,000 in 2010.

171. *BDE*, May 1, 1891, 6; Howard, *Eagle and Brooklyn*, 918–19; *PSHDDR*, 13.

172. Manbeck, "Historically Speaking."

173. Rice, *Reminiscences of Abraham Lincoln*, 637; *NYT*, April 5, 1928, 1.

174. Depew, *My Memories*, 374–76; *BDE*, April 25, 1892, 4.

175. Champlin, *Orations, Addresses and Speeches*, 8.

176. *BDE*, April 24, 1893, 1.

177. *NYT*, April 23, 1899, 2.

178. Ross and Pelletreau, *History of Long Island*, 287; *BDE*, January 9, 1917, 4.

179. *NYT*, December 25, 1892, 5.

180. Ibid., November 15, 1894, 16.

181. As of 2008, the Polytechnic Institute of NYU.

182. *BDE*, June 2, 1902, 5.

183. Ibid., March 9, 1904, 12.

184. Ibid., April 20, 1904, 9; March 12, 1995, 6; *NYTR*, March 12, 1905, 10.

185. Ibid., January 9, 1917, 4; *NYTR*, January 10, 1917, 13.

186. Ibid., October 25, 1917, 4.

187. Ibid., February 18, 1894, 20.

188. Burrows and Wallace, *History of New York City*, 1228.

CHAPTER 7

189. *NYT*, June 23, 1889, 8; *NYTR*, August 18, 1889, 3; September 1, 1889, 14; May 12, 1890, 12; November 23, 1890, 20; November 30, 1890, 9; September 6, 1891, 22.

190. Howard, *Eagle and Brooklyn*, 1012.

191. *NYTR*, July 4, 1889, 10; *BDE*, October 20, 1889, 1; *RERBG* 44, no. 1112 (July 6, 1889), 946; Broderick, *Triumvirate*, 371–72; Roth, *Architecture of McKim, Mead & White*, 162.

192. *NYTR*, August 18, 1889, 3.

193. Various sizes are actually noted: *NYT*, April 6, 1896, 6, lists the ring at 200 by 150 feet; 190 by 95 feet in King, *King's Views of New York*, 61; and 180 by 90 feet in *NYT*, April 13, 1893, 2.

194. *BDE*, November 19, 1890, 6; January 31, 1891, 6; *NYTR*, November 17, 1890, 1; November 23, 1890, 20; *NYT*, December 3, 1890, 8.

195. *NYT*, December 10, 1897, 11. He was granted clemency in 1897.

196. *BDE*, February 23, 1893, 2; April 9, 1893, 3; April 10, 1893, 4; April 13, 1893, 2; April 14, 1893, 5; April 16, 1893, 2; *Harper's Weekly*, May 13, 1893, 0 450ac; Brooklyn Riding and Driving Club, *Riding and Driving*.

197. *NYT*, April 13, 1893, 2.

198. *BDE*, April 16, 1893, 2.

199. *NYT*, April 24, 1926, 15.

200. Ibid., October 21, 1894, 12; April 6, 1896, 6.

201. Ibid., June 12, 1895, 6); *BDE*, July 21, 1895, 5.

202. *NYTR*, December 31, 1905, B6.

203. *BDE*, July 21, 1937, 15; *NYT*, July 21, 1937, 21; Space, *Cullen and Dykman*, 77–82.

204. *NYTR*, January 26, 1919, A7.

205. *Brooklyn Eagle*, January 15, 1939, 15A.

206. Horace, Odes (III.2.13).

207. *NYT*, May 3, 1922, 34; May 8, 1922, 16.

208. Ibid., June 6, 1925, 1, 2; June 8, 1925, 14; *WaPo*, June 6, 1925, 3.

209. *NYT*, June 6, 1925, 2.

210. Ibid., June 9, 1925, 12.

211. Ibid., June 10, 1925, 25.

212. Ibid., April 9, 1926, 14.

213. *BDE*, January 17, 1926, 1, 4; *NYT*, January 20, 1926, 4.

214. Laffaye, *Polo Encyclopedia*, 318; Laffaye, *Polo in the United States*, 225–27; Frank, *Jew in Sports*, 172.

215. Smith, "Heroes and Hurrahs," 10; Friedman, "Brooklyn Riding and Driving Club."

216. *BDE*, June 21, 1889, 6.

217. Ibid., November 14, 1893, 12; November 15, 1893, 8.

218. Ibid., August 6, 1939, B7. Originally located at the corner of Atlantic and Bedford Avenues.

CHAPTER 8

219. *NYT*, December 17, 1960, 8; O'Hanlon, "Neighborhood Change," 151ff.

220. O'Hanlon, "Neighborhood Change," 163–64.

221. *NYT*, October 23, 1927, W20.

222. *BDE*, August 19, 1945, 56.

223. Ibid., December 6, 1919, 1.

224. *NYT*, December 10, 1926, 23; April 2, 1927, 5; April 8, 1927, 1; March 3, 1928, 32.

225. *Brooklyn Eagle*, January 11, 1939, 1, 3; *NYT*, January 12, 1939, 39.

226. Kapsales, "From the Gilded Age," 116.

227. Ierardi, *Gravesend*, 144.

228. *NYT*, July 14, 1951, 15.

229. Osman, *Invention of Brownstone Brooklyn*, 218, states 1974; c.f. Wood, "Insuring Townhouse Living," 3–5; http://www.brownstoneagency.com.

230. *NYT*, December 26, 1974, 74; January 7, 1975, 24; November 14, 1982, R1; September 7, 2006, C17.

231. Though five other clubhouses survive: that of the Athletic (now the St. Anne's School), Brooklyn (a synagogue), Carleton (condos), Lincoln (Mechanics Temple, United Order of Mechanics) and Union (a senior citizen's home). *NYT*, September 11, 1994, CY12; August 12, 2010, RE7.

Bibliography

Black, David. *The King of Fifth Avenue*. New York: Dial Press, 1981.

Bowen, Edward L. "James Rowe Sr." In *Masters of the Turf: Ten Trainers Who Dominated Racing's Golden Age*. Lexington, KY: Eclipse Press, 2007.

Broderick, Mosette. *Triumvirate: McKim, Mead & White: Art, Architecture, Scandal, and Class in America's Gilded Age*. New York: Alfred A. Knopf, 2010.

Brooklyn Life. "The Montauk Club." May 25, 1915.

Brooklyn Riding and Driving Club. *The Riding and Driving Club's First Annual Horseshow*. Brooklyn, NY: Brooklyn Riding and Driving Club, 1893.

Burrows, Edwin G., and Mike Wallace. *A History of New York City to 1898*. Oxford, UK: Oxford University Press, 1999.

Champlin, John Denison, ed. *Orations, Addresses and Speeches of Chauncey M. Depew*. Vol. 3, *Birthday and Anniversary Addresses*. New York: privately printed, 1910.

Cudahy, Brian. *How We Got to Coney Island: The Development of Mass Transportation in Brooklyn and King's County*. New York: Fordham University Press, 2002.

Cullen, Frank et al. *Vaudeville Old & New. An Encyclopedia of Variety Performers in America*. Vol. 2. New York: Routledge, 2007.

Das Deutsche Element der Stadt New York : Biographisches Jahrbuch der Deutsch-Amerikaner New Yorks und Umgebung. New York: Spengler, 1913.

Depew, Chauncey Mitchell. *My Memories of Eighty Years*. New York: Charles Scribner's Sons, 1924.

Ditta, Joseph. *Gravesend, Brooklyn*. Charleston, SC: Arcadia Publishing, 2009.

Frank, Stanley. *The Jew in Sports*. New York: Miles Publishing Company, 1936.

Friedman, Florence Z. "Brooklyn Riding and Driving Club." Main Collection, Brooklyn Historical Society.

Gaynor, William Jay. *Some of Mayor Gaynor's Letters and Speeches*. New York: Greaves Publishing Company, 1913.

Horan, James D., and Howard Swiggett. *The Pinkerton Story*. New York: G.P. Putnam's Sons, 1951.

Howard, Henry D.B., ed. *The Eagle and Brooklyn: The Record of the Progress of the* Brooklyn Daily Eagle; *Issued in Commemoration of Its Semi-Centennial and Occupancy of Its New Building; Together with the History of the City of Brooklyn*. Brooklyn, NY: Brooklyn Daily Eagle, 1893.

Ierardi, Eric J. *Gravesend, the Home of Coney Island*. New York: Vantage Press, 1975.

Jarman, Rufus. "The Great Racetrack Caper." *American Heritage* 19, no. 5 (August 1968): 24–27, 92–94.

Kapsales, Maria A. "From the Gilded Age to Progressivism: Brooklyn's Horse Race for Wealth." MA thesis, City University of New York, 1990.

Kartalis, Betty. "Percy William's Legacy." *Shore Lines* (June 1986): 3, 10.

King, Moses. *King's Views of New York, 1896–1915 & Brooklyn, 1905*. New York: Arno Press, 1974.

Laffaye, Horace A. *The Polo Encyclopedia*. Jefferson, NC: McFarland & Company, Inc., 2004.

———. *Polo in the United States: A History*. Jefferson, NC: McFarland & Company, Inc., 2011.

Lancaster, Paul. *Gentleman of the Press: The Life and Times of an Early Reporter, Julian Ralph, of the* Sun. Syracuse, NY: Syracuse University Press, 1992.

Liebman, Bennett. "Horseracing in New York in the Progressive Era." *Gaming Law Review and Economics* 12, no. 6 (2008): 550–62.

Manbeck, John. "Historically Speaking: Brooklyn Day, All the Way." *Brooklyn Daily Eagle*, June 8, 2011. http://www.brooklyneagle.com/archive/category.php?category_id=15&id=43923.

McCullough, Edo. *Good Old Coney Island*. 2nd ed. New York: Fordham University Press, 2000.

The Memorial Cyclopedia of the Twentieth Century, Comprising Memoirs of Men and Women Who Have Been Instrumental in the Progress of the Industries, Professions, Arts, Literature, Legislation, Society and Charities of the United States. New York: Publishing Society, 1906.

Montauk Club, Brooklyn. New York: New York Engraving and Printing Company, 1890.

Morn, Frank. *The Eye That Never Sleeps: A History of the Pinkerton National Detective Agency*. Bloomington: Indiana University Press, 1982.

Morrone, Francis. *An Architectural Guidebook to Brooklyn*. Layton, UT: Gibbs Smith, 2001.

———. *Park Slope Neighborhood & Architectural History Guide*. Brooklyn, NY: Brooklyn Historical Society, 2008.

The New York City Landmarks Preservation Commission. *Park Slope Historic District Designation Report*. New York: New York City Landmarks Preservation Commission, 1973.

O'Hanlon, Timothy. "Neighborhood Change in New York City: A Case Study of Park Slope, 1850–1980." PhD diss., City University of New York, 1982.

Osman, Suleiman. *The Invention of Brownstone Brooklyn: Gentrification and the Search for Authenticity in Postwar New York.* Cary, NC: Oxford University Press USA, 2011.

Park Slope Civic Council. "Garrison's Finish: See Where the Jockey Lived Who Helped Bring Park Slope in a Winner." *Park Slope Civic Council Civic News* 71, no. 8 (April 2009): 1, 6.

———. "Tales Along the House Tour: Marriage and Divorce, Life and Death." *Park Slope Civic Council Civic News* 70, no. 9 (May 2008): 1, 4.

Pink, Louis Heaton. *Gaynor: The Tammany Mayor Who Swallowed the Tiger.* New York: International Press, 1931.

Rice, Allen Thorndike. *Reminiscences of Abraham Lincoln by Distinguished Men of His Time.* New York: North American Publishing Company, 1886.

Riess, Steven A. *The Sport of Kings and the Kings of Crime: Horse Racing, Politics, and Organized Crime in New York, 1865–1913.* Syracuse, NY: Syracuse University Press, 2011.

Robertson, William H.P. *The History of Thoroughbred Racing in America.* New Jersey: Prentice-Hall, Inc., 1964.

Rogers, Will. *The Papers of Will Rogers: Wild West and Vaudeville: April 1904– September 1908.* Edited by Arthur Frank Wertheim and Barbara Bair. Oklahoma City: Oklahoma University Press, 2000.

Ross, Peter, and William S. Pelletreau. *A History of Long Island, from Its Earliest Settlement to the Present Time.* Vols. 1–3. New York: Lewis Publishing Company, 1903.

Roth, Leland M. *The Architecture of McKim, Mead & White, 1870–1920.* New York: Garland Reference Library of the Humanities, 1978.

Schwartz, David G. *Roll the Bones: The History of Gambling*. New York: Gotham Books, 2006.

Smith, Mortimer. *William Jay Gaynor, Mayor of New York*. Chicago: Henry Regnery Company, 1951.

Smith, Robert P. "Heroes and Hurrahs: Sports in Brooklyn, 1890–1898." *Journal of Long Island History* 11, no. 2 (1975): 7–21.

Space, Fred L. *Cullen and Dykman: Past and Present*. Brooklyn, NY: Cullen and Dykman, 1955.

Stewart, Travis (aka Trav S.D.). *No Applause—Just Throw Money: The Book That Made Vaudeville Famous*. New York: Faber and Faber, Inc., 2005.

Thomas, Lately. *The Mayor Who Mastered New York: The Life & Opinions of William J. Gaynor*. New York: William Morrow & Company, Inc., 1969.

Trager, James. *The New York Chronology: The Ultimate Compendium of Events, People, and Anecdotes from the Dutch to the Present*. New York: HarperCollins, 2003.

Vamplew, Wray. "Sporting Innovation: The American Invasion of the British Turf and Links, 1895–1905." *Sport History Review* 35 (2004): 122–37.

Vosburgh, W.S. *Racing in America, 1866–1921*. New York: Jockey Club, 1922.

Wood, Claire. "Insuring Townhouse Living." *Old-House Journal* 2, no. 12 (December 1974): 3–5.

INDEX

ABOUT THE AUTHOR

Lucas Rubin is the director of the Sports Management Program at Columbia University. With a PhD in Classics from the University of Buffalo, he has lived on Sportsmen's Row since 2003.

Visit us at
www.historypress.net